A WORLD WITHOUT TEARS

A WORLD WITHOUT TEARS

The CASE OF CHARLES ROTHENBERG

HARRY J. GAYNOR,
JACK WILSON,
AND ANDREW SAVICKY

PRAEGER

New York
Westport, Connecticut
London

Library of Congress Cataloging-in-Publication Data

Gaynor, Harry J.
  A World without tears.

  1. Rothenberg, Charles.   2. Abusive parents—
United States—Biography.   I. Wilson, Jack, Rev.
II. Savicky, Andrew.
HV6248.R69G39   1990   362.7'6'092   [B]   89-71193
  ISBN 0-275-93693-7

Library of Congress Catalog Card Number: 89-71193
ISBN: 0-275-93693-7

First published in 1990

Praeger Publishers, One Madison Avenue, New York, NY 10010
An imprint of Greenwood Publishing Group, Inc.

Printed in the United States of America

The paper used in this book complies with the
Permanent Paper Standard issued by the National
Information Standards Organization (Z39.48-1984).

10 9 8 7 6 5 4 3 2 1

Contents

vii Preface
ix Book Rationale
xi Note
xiii Statement

INTRODUCTION
1 Harry Gaynor
18 Jack Wilson
20 Andrew Savicky

CHARLES ROTHENBERG
22 *The Early Years*
30 *Transition*
40 *Living on the Edge*

ANALYSIS I
63 Jack Wilson
67 Andrew Savicky

CHARLES ROTHENBERG
71 *Struggles*

ANALYSIS II
88 Jack Wilson
90 Andrew Savicky

CHARLES ROTHENBERG
93 *Tragedy*

ANALYSIS III
113 Jack Wilson
119 Andrew Savicky
Child Abuse Formula
123 Harry Gaynor
Summary

APPENDIX
Andrew Savicky
124 Human Figure
Drawings
130 Complete the Sentence
Test

Harry Gaynor
132 Parental Factors
in Child Abuse
133 Risk Factors
in Abused Children

134 **HELP INFORMATION**

135 **UPDATE ON CHARLES
ROTHENBERG**

136 **ABOUT THE AUTHORS**

Preface

Charles Rothenberg committed an unthinkable crime — he deliberately set fire to the bed where his six-year-old son, David, lay sleeping. Though David did not die, his burns covered 90 percent of his body and left him severely disfigured. These are the facts: indisputable, incontrovertible, horrible.

Charles Rothenberg admitted his guilt and spent seven years in prison with his release scheduled for 1990. These, too, are facts.

But one can hardly even read the words without a visceral reaction.

Questions clamor for answers. How could he...? Why did he...? What if...? What next...? And here the facts are not so readily available.

This book is an attempt to reach behind the facts, to enter the mind and the emotions of Charles Rothenberg, to gain some understanding of what led up to his crime, and, most important, to employ that understanding in protecting other children of other parents from abuse.

The core of this book is the in-depth study of Charles through over 140 letters, personal interviews and his own writings. Some of these revelations weave a tale that stands outside conventional reality. Must we accept it as truth? Is he a victim himself? Yes. No. Maybe...

Some of his words offer real and painful insights into human emotion and human behavior. Do patterns emerge? Can we catch glimpses of ourselves? Possibly. Sometimes...

The study of Charles reveals a troubled life and, perhaps, lessons to be learned and applied.

Commenting about Charles Rothenberg are Harry J. Gaynor, a recognized authority on child abuse by burning and President of the National Burn Victim Foundation; the Rev. Dr. Jack Wilson, a minister and counselor, and Senior Pastor of Calvary Evangelical Free Church in Essex Fells, New Jersey; and Dr. Andrew Savicky, a psychologist and Psychology Director at the Southern State Correctional Facility in Delmont, New Jersey.

From their professional perspectives, these authors offer an analysis of the mystery that is Charles Rothenberg. ■

Book Rationale

I can assure the reader that I spent many restless nights thinking about whether the National Burn Victim Foundation, or I, as its founder, should have anything to do with a book about Charles Rothenberg. Why, I asked myself, would anyone want to read a book about this child abuser? It was a sick situation and I didn't think I had the stomach for it, much less to place the Foundation's excellent reputation in jeopardy.

There were risks; risks that the media and our peers might not look beyond the crime and the man, whom even staunch Christians despised. Emotional public reaction against Rothenberg could impact negatively on the National Burn Victim Foundation, and the Foundation might not survive.

Every day our dedicated staff has to live with child abuse by burning incidents. Together we have to face violence perpetrated on children about which the public seldom hears.

Child abuse by burning is like a runaway train, traveling so fast that it misses the signals along the way. Our objective is to slow down the train, or the children on board will be abandoned and many will themselves continue the cycle of violence. Whatever price we have to pay we will pay, as long as we do not forget our objectives: to save a child; to save a parent. If we can accomplish those objectives, the risks were worthwhile.

This is a powerful story. We can and will survive the emotional response, and child abuse prevention will have taken a step forward.

I wish to thank the Foundation's staff: Norma C. Godin, R.N., Thomas Duffy, and Gail Allen who were constant reminders of our objective; and my family and friends who told me, "If you really want to stop that runaway train you have to stick your neck out." God, do I want to stop that train!

Harry J. Gaynor

▨ Note

The names of several of the people whom Charles Rothenberg knew at various times in his life have been changed in order to protect their privacy. The National Burn Victim Foundation wishes the reader to note that neither Dr. Savicky nor Dr. Wilson were Charles Rothenberg's personal therapists or counselors, and their views are representative of their individual interviews with Charles Rothenberg and studies of his manuscript and letters. Further, Charles Rothenberg's views of the world and his various interactions with numerous people represent those of Charles Rothenberg and are not representative of the views of the National Burn Victim Foundation or any of the authors other than Charles Rothenberg.

All royalties from this book have been waived by the authors, and have been designated to benefit the National Burn Victim Foundation's child abuse programs and services.

Statement

I pray this book will help other parents to recognize and to avoid situations and circumstances which can contribute to the abuse of their children. I know this book will save some children from harm.

I know this book will surely wake people up about child abuse, and that the National Burn Victim Foundation's work throughout the United States in child abuse and neglect will be expanded to see that there is never another David Rothenberg incident or a father or mother who would cause such pain and suffering to their child as I have done to my own son.

My son, David, must live disfigured and deprived of all that life could have given him because of me, and I must live with myself knowing how I hurt my son I love. I cannot tell you or even find the words to explain the pain that is in my heart. I do not ask for forgiveness, I cannot forgive myself. Only through Jesus Christ who died for my sins can I live in this world.

I want this book to expand the National Burn Victim Foundation's endeavors in child abuse and neglect, and to reach and help children here in the United States and around the world so that my son's pain will not have been in vain.

Charles D. Rothenberg

A WORLD WITHOUT TEARS

Introduction
Harry Gaynor

March 4, 1983 was a cold morning. Even before I put on the coffee pot, I headed for my driveway where the daily newspaper, as usual, had been tossed under my car. I cannot understand why I am always so eager to see what is in the newspaper. Rarely does the news brighten my day. That morning was no exception; there, glaring at me from the front page, was the headline, "Father Torches His Son."

My gut reaction was that they should give this guy the same treatment. What could possess a father to burn his own son? Only one answer was possible—something went wrong inside his head. He had to be crazy. No decent, sane person would do such a thing to any child, much less his son!

Newscasters were giving updates on the story throughout the day. The family was from Brooklyn; the boy's parents were divorced. Without telling his ex-wife, the father, Charles Rothenberg, had sneaked his son, David, off to California presumably to visit Disneyland.

Then, the unimaginable happened—he set fire to the bed in which David lay sleeping. David was horribly burned and probably would not live.

New York police already had a warrant for Charles Rothenberg's arrest on charges of stealing from his employer. It was also reported that he had served time in prison for writing bad checks, was suspected of being an arsonist, and had now apparently attempted to burn his son to death. The emotion I felt was strong.

Millions of people were no doubt following this story with varying degrees of shock and concern. The sensational always makes us sit up and take notice, and an account of a father burning his son was, at the very least, bizarre. But as founder and president of the National Burn Victim Foundation, I had a particular interest.

Thousands of children in the United States are accidentally burned every year. I have met hundreds of parents whose children sustained severe burns. Burn patients seldom suffer alone; their families suffer along with them. But David was intentionally burned.

When I see guilt-ridden parents torture themselves over an act of carelessness that resulted in their child's being burned, I find it hard to believe that a father would use fire as the means to destroy his son. There had to be more to it. The accounts were full of assumptions and speculation. I thought about the number of false charges of child abuse being made against parents. Maybe I just didn't want to believe this incredible story.

Charles Rothenberg was being hunted, wanted for the attempted murder of his son. If David died, Charles would face a murder charge. Hastily produced "Wanted" posters appeared everywhere. Buena Park, California, police were taking no chances, providing 24-hour protection for David and his mother, Marie. Perhaps Charles would try to finish the job when he learned that his son was still alive. Reports surfaced that Charles had tried to kill his son by fire on two other occasions, but he was never charged for lack of evidence.

The police department and area newspapers were receiving tips from people who thought they knew Charles' whereabouts. However, when Marie saw one of the posters, she was said to have screamed, "That is not Charles." The sketch came from descriptions by several people who had seen Charles at the Buena Park Motel, and there was little, if any, similarity between Charles and the sketch on the posters. They were hunting the wrong man. New posters were made from photographs, and Charles' face appeared on TV and in newspapers in and around Orange County, California.

The police disclosed that a man identifying himself as David's father had called, making inquiries about David, the extent of his burns, and his prognosis. He probably used many aliases in trying to find out about David's condition. This behavior was strange for a father who had attempted to murder his son, but then everything about this father was strange.

On one occasion Charles agreed to turn himself in to the police but didn't keep his promise. Several days later he sent a telegram stating that by the time they got the message he would be out of the country. He had a history of being a convincing liar.

Eight days after Charles set fire to his son, the police arrested him outside a San Francisco YMCA. He was calm and made no attempt to resist. Charles was transferred to Orange County the following day where he was to be jailed and tried for the attempted murder of his son. He continued to show concern, asking for information about David's condition and Marie's welfare.

Prisoners have their own code of justice, and Charles' safety was cause for concern. Inmates hate child abusers, as many were themselves victims of abuse. Charles was therefore isolated from other prisoners.

Charles confessed that he did, indeed, try to murder his son. Marie testified for the prosecution, telling the court about her life with Charles, about his lying and getting into trouble with the law. She also told the court about how jealous Charles was of the time her fiance, New York City police officer John Cirillo, spent with David.

Charles' attorney recommended basing his defense on a plea of insanity, but Charles refused. He also refused to be interviewed by psychiatrists.

It was an open and shut case; only a guilty verdict was possible. The presiding judge said he wished he could give Charles a life sentence, but by law the longest sentence he could impose was thirteen years. Spectators gasped.

When asked by the judge whether he had anything to say, Charles consulted his notes and said, "I'd like to now ask your forgiveness, as I have forgiven you both. I will have to live with what I have done as long as I live, and Marie and John, you will have to live with a disfigured child for as long as he lives."

David sustained third degree burns over 90 percent of his body surface. Rule-of-thumb guidelines put his chances for survival at about 4 percent - not very good odds. He was fortunate to be hospitalized at the University of California Burn Center, where he had a fighting chance. Most children with such extensive burns die, but David proved to be the exception. He did, however, lose his fingers, toes, and ears and would be disfigured for the rest of his life. The quality of his life was destroyed by his father.

It is not easy for disfigured people to live in our beauty-oriented society, which has standards of acceptable appearance. Those falling below the norm often suffer rejection. David's journey through life will not be an easy one. Both David and Charles will live their lives with the question of "why" haunting them. Charles' nightmares will not be as he sleeps, but each new day, as he looks into the mirror and questions himself.

Charles was transferred to Soledad Prison, known to be a tough prison housing criminals who had committed murder and other violent crimes. Once again Charles lived in solitary confinement for his own safety. If he was in danger from inmates at Orange County Prison, then he was surely a marked man at Soledad.

Public attention to David and Charles slowly waned, but interest revived when the story resurfaced from time to time. David was making reasonable progress. His attitude was fantastic; the sensationalism surrounding his burn injury was over. David's visit to Disneyland made some news, and his transfer in 1983 to the Shriners Burns Institute in Boston also received media coverage.

In 1985 Marie Rothenberg wrote a book called David, co-authored by Mel White. It was Marie's story about her life with Charles, the tragedy of Charles' crime, and David's brave struggle to survive and overcome. ABC-TV produced and broadcast a movie based on this book two years later. Still there were no answers to the big question—Why?

In March 1985, the producer of the Phil Donahue Show called to ask if I would appear on a television program in April that would focus on how people react to burn victims and others with visible disfigurement. I suggested instead inviting Anthony Luppino, Ph.D., a psychologist who had been massively burned and was director of the Foundation's Burn Crisis Intervention Team. His input, I assured the producer, would have an impact. Much to my surprise, I learned that David Rothenberg and his mother would also be on the program.

The show aired on April 3, 1985, and Donahue skillfully elicited the feelings and experiences of the participants. At the end of the program, the National Burn Victim Foundation's address and telephone number were flashed on the screen. The telephone began to ring in our office, and within days mail came in from around the country.

Among the letters was one from Charles D. Rothenberg:

April 9, 1985

Charles David Rothenberg,
C-70536
Soledad Prison
P.O. Box 689
(CTF-Central-PHU-1-136L)
Soledad, California
93960-0689

Chairperson In-Charge
National Burn Victim Foundation
308 Main Street
Orange, New Jersey 07050

Re: Confidential

Dear Sir or Madam:

I am the father to David Rothenberg, the burn victim you have read about, and reached national attention.

My letter to you is painful! And regardless of what you may or may not personally feel about me concerning this unwanted tragedy, one I thought would never occur, but did, I, too, have to live with this as a father.

This brief correspondence is to ask if I, as David's father, can assist him in some way, donating some skin, parts of my anatomy to relieve his pain for reconstruction? I am certainly unable to contribute on a financial basis, at least until my ultimate release in '89. I wish I could!

I could never justify or excuse myself for this act, regardless of the true events still untold. The hardest part for me is to forgive myself. It has been difficult. I love David, and will say no more. If I could help him, I would - and other burn victims - as the father of a burn victim -

4

to raise funds for your foundation. I just never thought so much publicity would come about, and as of today I am subject to telling "my side" of the story. Your address was given to me by someone working for the "Donahue Show."

Sincerely,
Charles D. Rothenberg

I read the letter a number of times. My first reaction was to tear it up and throw it in the round file. Our Foundation was dedicated to burn victims; what could we offer Charles Rothenberg, a man who admitted he had burned his own son?

Some of his words reached out to me, especially *"...the hardest part for me is to forgive myself."* How could this man even think about forgiving himself? *"I love David and will say no more."* What did he mean by that? My curiosity was really aroused by his words, *"true events still untold."*

When I first became involved with the problems associated with child abuse and neglect by burning in 1975, I recognized the importance of suspects' statements - what they said, when they said it, and why they said it. Whether it was an impulsive, one-time act of violence or repeated abuse of a child, the suspects' words, when matched with forensic evidence, would lead to the truth about how the burn injury happened.

In the more than 900 suspected child abuse by burning cases with which I have been involved, a significant number of suspects lied or evaded answers, making up stories to bolster their version of what happened. Forensic evidence doesn't lie or evade questions—only people lie.

This man committed one of the most outrageous crimes conceivable against his own flesh and blood. What could I learn from Charles Rothenberg that I did not already know from the 900 cases documented? What was his history? Was he abused as a child? Knowing more about Charles might only reconfirm what we had already identified in research, but perhaps, just perhaps, Charles would open up a new direction in analyzing suspects' backgrounds.

On April 19, 1985, I decided to write to Charles Rothenberg. I told him that his son no longer needed donor skin and that there was little he could do to help David. I told him that I surely could not forgive him; however, if he was really sorry for his crime, I might understand how painful it was for him to live with himself. I told him I would pray for David ... and for him.

Charles' violent act and subsequent actions were unique. Those who commit child abuse by burning usually claim they do not know how the injury occurred or manufacture stories they feel are believable. Even in homicide cases, the perpetrator often claims innocence and sticks with the story originally told to investigators.

So many answers were needed to fit together the puzzle that was Charles Rothenberg. I felt challenged to dig into this man's mind, to know him perhaps better than any other person. If through Charles I could discover a single answer that would spare some child pain or death, it would be worth my time and effort. Little did I realize that within the next four years I would receive over 140 letters from Charles Rothenberg.

In his second letter Charles enclosed a poem he said he had written on June 18, 1983: "A World Without Tears" (see poem on page 107.)

Was he thinking about what he had done to David? To Marie? To himself? Was he wishing that he could live his life over again? Is he saying he doesn't want to cry any more? Does he want to die?

I was still somewhat uncomfortable with this correspondence. I knew the direction I wanted to take, but wondered if Charles would be honest with me. According to Marie he was a pathological liar. I decided to write a very strong letter, letting him know where I stood, and challenging him to be forthright. I had nothing to lose.

If he tried to blame someone else for what he did to his son, I would assume that he was still mentally sick, that he was looking for excuses and attempting to justify his violent act. With all of the positive things I could be doing to help burn victims, I didn't want to waste time playing games with Charles.

Charles wrote again. His letter gave me better insight:

June 4, 1985

Dear Mr. Gaynor:

Your letter of 5/30 reached me today, and I was happy to hear from you. Your letter was straight to the point, up front, and I expect to be the same way in corresponding with you.

You mentioned you detected in my letter and the book David, that I have or seek justification of my actions on "that day." This is not true! I already had a chance when Mel White co-author of David, wanted to come from New York, after spending five and a half weeks with Marie, writing the book for her. He called here and explained to the department spokesperson that he felt there was more to this story. I decided not to see him. You said it yourself in your letter: "I cannot conceive in my mind how anyone could ever forgive himself under such circumstances." I would never justify this terrible act I committed. I cannot get over "my son's physical condition. And this is the bottom line." I see David "then" and "now." I am his father, Mr. Gaynor, and I do have a conscience ... very much so. This is why I am going through

6

a difficult time with myself. I am dealing with myself and the reality of the true situation. I even accept the "lot" you mentioned. It is going to take time to come to total grips with it all. I ask God for help in my personal plight, and I feel, with His help in time, I will "enter the door with both feet." If I were to tell you differently, Mr. Gaynor, that I have, it would be a lie.

I would very much like to continue to correspond with you. Your letters are "straight to the point." "You pull no punches!" It helps me deal with "today", and I can better come to grips with all this through your honesty, and by prayer, which I do a lot of.

It is not easy for me to say how shameful I am over "why" I'm incarcerated. I am! I pray "David" my son, will forgive me ... I truly hope we can get to know each other, and you would want to help me come to the Lord, and just be yourself - as you are - continuing to give me good words, in order that I may one day be set free from within.

Most Sincerely
Charles

I was moved by his response. I wanted to believe him, but I suspected he might be using me, possibly hoping I would speak on his behalf at some future parole hearing. Nonetheless, our correspondence continued.

His letters were full of emotion - crying out, *"I want to see my son,"* and *"I want to ask David to forgive me."* If indeed Charles Rothenberg was insane at the time he burned his son and today he is rational, he must be tortured by guilt. I asked him if he was blaming Marie for his crime against David. *"No, I have only myself to blame. Marie was a good mother to my son,"* he said. But then he would talk about *"Marie's mouth"* and how she was always putting him down. *"Her mouth,"* he said, *"would never shut up."*

He said Marie had denied that there was a custody fight for David. It was a bitter fight, he wrote, and he sent a copy of a letter from his attorney (Roy Cohn from the McCarthy era—famous and wealthy) to prove his statement. Other letters from attorneys indicated that Charles was being asked to give David up for adoption to Marie's fiance, John. Charles said he never had a father, and he would not do to David what had been done to him. *"Life without a father,"* he wrote, *"was empty."*

He told me about the Chapmans, a Christian family who befriended him when he was in Orange County Prison. He said that in 1983 he accepted the Lord and became a born-again Christian. I asked about his conversion: when he "knocked on the door" (meaning asked Jesus Christ into his life), did the door open and did he step in? He answered that he could only get one foot in. This admission seemed honest, and it encouraged me to dig further.

I wrote to Charles about my frustration in trying to educate the public and those in government agencies responsible for the safety and welfare of children about child abuse/neglect by burning. So many children needed help, and the Foundation's funds were limited.

Charles said in his letters that it was painful for him to think about these children, and he questioned why parents and guardians would do such things to their children. Like everything else worthwhile in this world, I told him, it takes money to make things happen.

My comments inspired Charles to write to politicians such as Senator Ted Kennedy and Congressman Leon Panetta, asking that they help the National Burn Victim Foundation. He even attempted to get a fund-raiser going at Soledad Prison, but without success. I received a long letter from Charles with well-thought-out ideas on how to raise money for the Foundation. Some were good ideas, but all took a lot of seed money.

Charles mentioned in one letter that someone had given him a typewriter and that he was writing a manuscript about his life. *"If you want it, Harry,"* he wrote, *"if you think my story would help prevent some child from being abused, or prevent some parent from making the same mistake I did, you can have it."* Neither Marie nor David wanted money, or anything in fact, from him, he noted.

This was an offer I could not refuse - his manuscript might fill in a lot of blank spaces. Writing a book about him was not foremost in my mind at the time, but I began to think about the possibility.

Charles wrote that the Chapman family offered to deliver a birthday card from him to David. They later told Charles that they believed David still loved him, although he was not yet ready to see his father.

As Charles wrote about this event, he was very excited. His spirits were high—David might still love him! He asked me how I thought he should handle a reunion with David. He was scared—unsure of how David would react.

Soon after, however, he received a message from Marie who asked him to let them be at peace and not to try to see David. David's words were, "You are not my father any more, and I don't love you."

Surprisingly, Charles was amenable: *"If that is what my son wants, then I will respect his wishes. I will make no attempt to see Marie or David unless they want to meet with me."* It was the first time Charles seemed to accept reality, to accept the fact that his son did not want to see him.

Charles often wrote about the interviews and letters he had received from ABC-TV personnel working on the movie, David. They visited him at Soledad and told him, he said, they were going to be more favorable toward him than Marie's book was.

Charles suggested to ABC that they contact the National Burn Victim Foundation for my comments because he had been corresponding with me and wished to help the Foundation.

ABC sent a crew to interview me for a news segment to follow the movie. The result of the interview was an innocuous few seconds on the air, but they did not report what was of paramount importance: neither I nor the National Burn Victim Foundation are advocates for Charles Rothenberg. We are advocates for his son.

The movie, David, however, was superb—an even-handed recounting of events based on Marie's book but with input from Charles as well. Charles said he was pleased with it but found it painful to watch.

Charles' letters kept on coming; much of what he wrote was repetitious, such as his acceptance of Jesus Christ into his life. Any reference to seeing his son he always capped with, *"if he wants to see me, Marie too."* What surprised me were his expressions of love for his ex-wife, Marie. He seemed to be softening his tone toward her, often stating that she was a good woman and a good mother to David.

Charles focused more on his parole in his letters, saying he was scared - scared of what is out in the world for him. He would not have a parole board review, he wrote, but California law dictated that he must leave prison.

In February, 1989, I received a telephone call from Steve Rodriguez, Charles' parole officer. He too was concerned about Charles' release and asked if I could help. Charles had made the same request a number of times. *"I'm scared. I have no family, no friends, and the world has changed so much. Please help me find a place to live; a job. I am a hard worker, a workaholic so to speak,"* Charles wrote. But there was more. Charles would not be welcome in California. The media had run story after story about David's progress since 1983.

Steve Rodriguez confirmed the ill feelings toward Charles and suggested that it would be best if he could find a place out of state. Charles thought he would like to live and work in a Christian community or with senior citizens. He wanted to prove to people, to David, and to himself that he could be a "good man." I made no promises beyond exploring some contacts.

On February 11, 1989, The Reporters, a Fox TV documentary program, was aired, showing flashbacks of the book David, some scenes from the ABC-TV movie, and an interview with Charles. The show was emotionally packed, and the interviewer had a field day with Charles.

Charles made it quite clear in his next letter that he didn't want any more media interviews. *"They tell you one thing just to get you to be a willing person to be interviewed, but when they get you on the camera it is a whole different story,"* he wrote. *"I had a lot of, at least*

I thought so, things I wanted to say. I thought people would like to know about my feelings. Instead the only thing they showed was me crying and saying I want to see my son."

You cannot communicate with someone for four years without feeling you know that person. We called each other "Mister" for three years; then in one letter I called him Charles. He immediately picked up on it and thereafter wrote to me as Harry. Sometimes I wished I had not initiated that intimacy, but what was done was done.

The time had come for me to face reality. I could not handle Charles all by myself. I needed help to think rationally about this man and not simply rely on my emotions.

I mentioned Charles' letter to the Rev. Dr. Jack Wilson, senior pastor of Calvary Evangelical Free Church in Essex Fells, New Jersey. Rev. Wilson is a man with a great deal of human insight who could put things into proper perspective. He surely was not naive about worldly events, nor easily shocked.

After church one Sunday I approached Rev. Wilson about Charles, asking him to read a few of Charles' letters. Rev. Wilson agreed, but said he would really have to think hard about a father who could do such a terrible thing to his son. The following Sunday Rev. Wilson said he would like to read more of Charles' letters. He, too, found the man a puzzle and the case appalling yet fascinating.

Ever since Charles offered his manuscript to me I had been pondering ways to use it, especially to shed some light into the dark corners of child abuse. Perhaps the manuscript could stand alone, but more likely it would need commentary and analysis. Certainly a psychological review would be essential. And with Charles' profession of Christianity, exploration from a spiritual perspective would be valuable. A book had taken shape in my mind.

I asked Rev. Wilson if he would be willing to co-author a book about Charles Rothenberg from the Christian viewpoint. He agreed immediately.

I next contacted Dr. Andrew Savicky, Psychology Director at the Southern State Correctional Facility, Delmont, New Jersey. I had met Dr. Savicky while I was lecturing on child abuse at the New Jersey State Police Academy. He was interested in the Foundation's use of forensics in evaluating child abuse by burning, and I felt he, too, might be interested in Charles.

When I asked him if he would join us in writing the book from the psychologist's view, he too agreed.

The following week Charles' manuscript arrived, and Rev. Wilson, Dr. Savicky and I met to formalize plans for the book. Charles was very excited at the prospect of publication. He reaffirmed his desire for the Foundation to benefit from sales of the book, and we co-authors agreed to volunteer our work, donating all royalties to support the National Burn Victim Foundation's burned child abuse/ neglect services and programs.

↘ Meanwhile Steve Rodriguez continued to call, pressuring me to find a place for Charles and stating that three months were needed to process paperwork if he was going to leave California. I was following up some promising leads, but he did not want to hear of problems - he wanted solutions.

A formal agreement was drawn up by our attorney and signed by the authors. We decided that we needed to meet Charles Rothenberg so that the reality of this man, and not just his words, would inform our writing. Everything began to move quickly, with Charles' release date pushing us into action. This book would be a formidable task.

Of 141 letters from Charles, totalling 283 pages, I believe his letters of February 1 and March 23, 1989, give us a fairly accurate view of Charles as he is today. The following excerpts are representative:

"I first want to-again-advise you that on Saturday, February 11th, Fox Network's The Reporters is airing nationwide and other parts of the world at a later date, a lengthy segment of me, David and Marie. The reporter who interviewed me and the producer said they feel my request to put your name, organization, address, and phone number on national TV is a very unselfish request. I pray they will do it."

They didn't put the sign up, nor did I expect they would. Media people, in an attempt to gain Charles' confidence, frequently make promises they have no intention of keeping. Charles, who is seeking acceptance, allows himself to be used again and again, although remaining suspicious of people.

"I also-again-want to ask you if you were interviewed because not only The Reporters, but many reporters around the country are asking me, 'Why don't you be a spokesperson for the National Burn Victim Foundation?' Now that I'm getting close to my ultimate release, the mail is really getting heavy, and only because I'm a bank book and rating to them all. Yet, the suggestion of me possibly being a spokesperson for your organization pleases me, and I just wondered if you know anything about this or have been contacted?"

The National Burn Victim Foundation could not permit Charles Rothenberg to be our spokesperson for obvious reasons. No one, to the best of my knowledge, is suggesting that he should assume that role.

"The docudrama David put a lot on my shoulders. People still want to know my side of the story-the-'truth.'"

Charles keeps coming back to the words, *"the truth."* I sense that he is hoping in some way to justify his violent act; that somehow society will understand why he did it, and therefore accept his action, without condoning it. The "truth" remains that Charles, by his own admission, deliberately set his son on fire for the purpose of murdering him.

"Even on Thursday, Jan. 26th, John Glover, the actor who portrayed me in David said to Jane Pauley, 'The most difficult role I've ever played was Charles Rothenberg.' They have been marketing John Glover for weeks now. Tomorrow he'll be on Pat Sajak's show on CBS. God I pray they won't put Glover up for an Emmy or exploit the motion picture. This would really put pressure on me."

Charles is missing the point. The interest up to now has not been Charles. He was the perpetrator, the source of ignition that propelled David into the limelight. His son then became a hero in the public eye. Charles must understand that child abusers can never be seen as heros.

"I'm in a critical situation, with no family, friends and very indigent. I do, though, have my clothes down in Whittier, California where a Christian family is holding them for me. Since I'm unable to live in that area because Marie and David live nearby, the Parole Agent suggested that I secure assistance out-of-state. He feels it would be easier to do my parole, as the crime happened in California."

Charles will present a problem for California, and he will do better as far away from David and Marie as possible. I sensed a rising panic in him not knowing what the future holds.

"I live with this tragedy every second of the day, and I will never get over what I have done to my son. I also feel very deeply for Marie, the mother of 'our son.' She has gone through a lot being with David from the beginning."

Throughout his letters he torments himself with the helplessness of his situation. He expresses his love for David and Marie. Child abusers violate a child in rage or in hate. Will David ever wonder if his father hated him, or in some strange way, loved him? Is it important that he should know?

"Do I drink, do drugs, play around, no, I was a workaholic to give David and Marie whatever they wanted or needed. I gave Marie a lot of things but I forgot about her emotional needs. I needed help and didn't know it. Then in a moment of weakness I destroyed my son's life."

Charles often repeats that he wants to be a good man, wants to prove himself to David and to society.

"If I had to do it all over again, what would I do differently or different: I think if I would have had the proper guidance as a child, brought up in a normal home, instead of an orphanage, living many times in the streets (homeless), mother being in show business, a prostitute, never knowing my real father, no brothers or sisters, I think this would, have made a difference in the way my life would have turned out. I reflect on so many things that made me go wrong in my life, much/most of which was my fault. Maybe I loved my son too much, maybe it was a selfish love?"

Most of us would do many things differently if we had the chance to do them over again. Charles Rothenberg would no doubt give anything to have the opportunity to change the course of that evening at the Buena Park Motel.

Child abusers are generally vindictive people; they inflict physical insults on a child for the purpose of causing the child pain. Their acts of violence may be the result of an utter dislike for the child, a form of revenge for their own bitterness against a spouse or live-in partner with the child as a scapegoat, or any of dozens of other reasons that are well documented in professional literature.

While we can now identify many similar traits of a child abuser with Charles, his crime is unique. Further, without knowing his background, he would not easily be identifiable as a potential child abuser.

"Many think I'm a push-over, as I always walk away when someone attacks me verbally. I hurt for others when I see them the way they are, and when they harm others verbally/physically."

While Charles does not say he was verbally abused as a child, his reference to his ex-wife's "mouth" suggests his inability to cope with verbal stress. Verbal family conflict has been identified as a trigger that often results in acts of violence against children.

"I've given a lot of thought about a name change a number of times. But I'm not sure of this. I must and will live in this world, and I don't want to ever be a coward again when I left my own son in that Motel room. People will say—if I change my name: 'he's still running.' I must and will face this entire situation head-on, with all the pain that will go along with it. I want my son, David, to know I do love him, and I want to ask David for his forgiveness someday, with God's guidance and help. I know you, Andy and Jack have read my mind and thoughts in the book you will now do. You will surely use the manuscript I sent

you. Yes, it's scary. I'm known around the world, and as I leave prison this year, it will even get worse. I believe I told you—if not—I received a letter from Tokyo, Japan. I turned them down after they asked me for an exclusive interview. They saw the docudrama David, and said to me, 'your wife pushed you to the brink.'

"There is no place for me to hide out there. Sooner or later someone would recognize me and I would be attacked verbally and perhaps physically. The media would then have another sensational story to report. If I had started a new life and was happy, I would be exposed and the story would start all over again. No, better I face whatever I have to."

Judging by his letters, Charles seems to have come to grips with his crime against his son. He does not want to be a coward—again. He does not want to run. Charles has been made aware of the problems he will face—rejection, disdain, contempt. He will be despised by a society that says he must suffer the rest of his life, that he must pay his debt beyond his prison term.

If he changed his name and his appearance, he could probably find a place to live and a job. So, then, why will he not change his name? Does he like the publicity and notoriety, being known, as he says, around the world? Realizing that he has a good chance of being physically harmed, even murdered, does he want to be punished? Does he have a death wish?

I believe that Charles is suffering deeply and that he feels ready to face the situation with all its accompanying pain. But he obviously has not yet learned that the media will manipulate him in order to get a story. Charles will continue to be visible until the sensationalism of his act is no longer of interest to the general public.

In late February, 1989, Rev. Wilson, Dr. Savicky, and I started making serious plans to fly to California to interview Charles at Soledad Prison. The meeting with Charles was vital; all three of us had a lot of questions to ask him—questions that could not be answered in letters. Dr. Savicky wanted to conduct several psychological tests, and we all wanted to tape Charles' conversation during our individual and collective meetings.

Arranging for the prison interview was complicated and frustrating. We filled out paperwork and obtained photo IDs. Not long before we were scheduled to go, Steve Rodriguez informed us that Charles was being transferred to the California Medical Facility at Vacaville. We sent duplicate paperwork there.

I received more calls from California authorities, asking me to help them in relocating Charles outside of California. I reiterated that I could not guarantee any of my resources would be able to take Charles, but Charles' letters continued to press for help to find a home on his release in December.

At the last minute we had to obtain special permission for a weekend interview: the rules were not the same at Soledad and Vacaville. Steve Rodriguez flew to Vacaville to meet us even though his wife had given birth to their son just the day before.

Steve seemed suspicious of our motives and wanted to know what we were going to do for Charles. He was pressing us for some commitment that seemed to me to be the responsibility of the State of California.

"We are not sure that this book is going to be good for Charles," Rodriguez stated.

"Steve," I said, "we are not going to do a 'job' on Charles Rothenberg. It is our mission to publish a book that will be helpful to parents, particularly parents who were themselves abused by a parent as children and thus are statistically more inclined to abuse their own children. It is also our goal to reach professionals who are involved with the health, protection and safety of children. We believe we can all learn much from Charles that will help us do a better job in the prevention and detection of child abuse by burning. While Charles' crime had to do with the burning of his son, what we hope to learn and share will be applicable to all abusive acts against children—not just burning."

"I hear what you're saying," replied Steve, "but Charles is a highly visible inmate, and when he walks out of prison, the media will be waiting—protestors as well. We are concerned for his safety, and the less attention paid to him the better."

I firmly stated, "This book is not going to harm Charles; in fact, I believe the public will have a better understanding of Charles. I could never be an advocate for him, or condone his crime, but the book will deliver a strong message to the public about what triggers the abuse of a child and how it can be avoided."

Security at Vacaville was intense. All 2,000 inmates were locked in their cells while Charles was brought from his solitary confinement. We learned that, as in Soledad, there were inmates who would like the recognition of being the one who "got" Charles Rothenberg. The prison authorities were taking no chances.

As we entered the interview room, Charles was sitting at a small table, hands folded. His face was expressionless, and he looked as if he had not slept. He was much thinner and looked older than he appeared on the TV interviews I had seen. In a soft voice he said, "I am glad you have come to see me." At first he seemed a bit uptight, as we all were, but he soon appeared relaxed and eager to answer our questions.

We interviewed Charles Rothenberg - both separately and together - for a total of ten hours that day. Charles had no lunch, nor did he request to use the bathroom during that time. The meeting room we used was air conditioned and frigid. Charles wore only a short-sleeved cotton prison shirt, and though his lips were blue and he trembled, he did not complain.

I spent the last hour with Charles going over what he had said in his letters. He assured me that everything was still true, with perhaps one exception. Putting his head in his hands, he said, "I prayed and believed that one day I would see my son. I kept believing I would hold him in my arms and ask his forgiveness; that he would say he forgave me, and that deep inside he loved me.

"Today I am resolved that I will never see David or Marie again in my lifetime. I can no longer hope for such a meeting with my son. His words to Marie when he was in the burn center, 'Why did Daddy want to hurt me?' will haunt me the rest of my life.

"I cannot change things for David or Marie, but I believe the story of my life will make parents stop and think before they hurt their children. They must learn now there is help for them. God, I wish there had been a source of help for me."

We were treated well overall by prison authorities. They cooperated with all of our requests and extended themselves by allowing us to remain for ten hours. The one unpleasant incident occurred when a guard removed film from Rev. Wilson's camera, even though we had authorization for its use, causing us to lose the pictures we hoped to use for this book. Otherwise the officials were friendly and cooperative.

Following my return from California, hardly a day went by without a letter (or two) from Charles regarding where he was going to live after his release. Charles repeatedly wrote that he was scared, that after seven years of solitary confinement he wasn't sure how he would fit into a society that hated him. He said he understood the hate because he hated himself for his crime. *"I pray that someone will help me,"* he wrote, *"I have no family, friends, no job to go to. With $200 in my pocket how will I survive?"*

Towards the end of July I received a collect call from Charles. He sounded panicky. "They have asked me to call, to tell you they must have an answer by August 15 whether you will or will not have a place for me."

I realized then that I was being dumped on, set up to be the scapegoat for California's failure to find an appropriate place for Charles to live outside that state.

"Harry," Charles said, "they say the book is going to be a great success, and I must be available to you for TV and other media people. They say if they have to keep me in California, I will not be available to the publisher or to the Foundation. If I am in another state, they say I will be able to move quickly whenever or wherever you want me."

The picture was becoming clearer. They, the California parole people, see Charles as a source of potential trouble. There was no safe place for Charles in California. Nonetheless, I wrote to Charles and Steve, clearly spelling out my position: neither I nor the Foundation would be responsible for Charles' rehabilitation.

I cannot help but wonder where Charles Rothenberg will end up. Prison is meant to rehabilitate the prisoner to return to society as a productive person. If society rejects the ex-prisoner and provides no place for him/her to live and work, then the system fails. There seems at this time to be no place for Charles. Can he survive in a world that has closed all its doors to him?

What we can believe is that, because of Charles' story, we will have taken a step forward in our fight against child abuse. ■

Jack Wilson

When Harry Gaynor first talked to me about Charles Rothenberg, my reaction was one of disgust. Why bother with someone who should be dead? Death is too good for anybody who can hurt his own kid like that. But then I knew that Harry was right: Charles was a human being. He had expressed some religious sentiment. And Harry wanted to minister to him. So I told Harry minister things to say and thought that would be the end of it.

But Charles wanted Harry to get his story published, and Harry asked me to contribute an evaluation of Charles from a religious point of view. Harry was insistent and persuasive. The authors wouldn't be making money — all royalties would go to the National Burn Victim Foundation — and such a book would contribute to human understanding of this special kind of suffering. And it seemed right.

The task at the outset had several things against it. For one, no real standard exists for testing the reality of religious experience. Many convicts and ex-convicts claim religious beliefs of one sort or another, but it appears that only time tells the reality of those claims. Secondly, Christian tradition has a built-in bias against judging others. Who is anyone to judge the sincerity of another's stated religious experience?

The difficulties are not insurmountable, though. Charles was asserting a religious experience within a certain defined religious context. He was claiming to be a Christian, one who had committed himself to the Jesus Christ of the historic Christian gospel. That gospel has definition. And it does describe and affirm the nature of life that follows repentance and faith.

Analytical questions might not be impossible after all. As for the judging part, people rightly assume when Jesus spoke out about judging ("Judge not that you be not judged"*) that he was speaking against such a practice. However, a closer look reveals that what he was getting at was the wrongness of a critical self-righteousness that so often characterizes followers of an old religious tradition. Reading further in the same passage ("Cast not your pearls before swine"), it's obvious that Jesus taught that some analysis is necessary, at least to determine the species of one's audience.

With these thoughts in mind, I planned several courses of evaluation when interviewing Charles and analyzing his manuscript and letters. I was curious about his religious background; the religious institutions he attended in his younger years; his early views of God; his views of the Bible; his experiences with key religious figures. I wanted to know about any changes in his thoughts about God and religion over the years; his understanding of Christ and the cross; his views of justice; how he was thinking through the memory of his crime.

I was interested in his conversion experience: when, where, and how often he had heard the gospel in his life; the main message he received from his conversion and his responses, both intellectual and emotional; his outlook after his conversion.

I wondered about his personal piety, his habits of Bible reading, prayer, and worship. I would attempt to understand his relationships with parent figures, for these relationships provide metaphors for one's developing concepts of God. And finally, I wanted to talk with him about his understanding of an important Christian concept that allows a person to live with him/herself, particularly after committing a horrendous act: that God has transferred the culpability for this act and for other sinful acts to Jesus Christ on the cross, so that in his death and resurrection, ordinary human beings receive perfect righteousness as a gift."

My hope for Charles was that through his Christian experience he would be able to find an avenue of understanding and wholeness as he faced life outside the prison walls. I hoped, too, that I might uncover some kernel of Christian truth that would help others before they reached the desperate state that causes them to lash out at a child. ■

_____

* Matthew 7:1,7:6
** II Corinthians 5:21

Andrew Savicky

The child who has been abused carries forever the mark of that cruelty and incorporates its effects into his/her adult persona. For those whose abuse was not so severe and who have other resources to overcome its influence, memory of the abuse merely lingers like a cold shadow in the dim recesses of the past. For others, the abuse spawns emotional distress on many levels and sometimes inappropriate actions. For still others, personality disorders, abuse of their own children, and other criminal acts that involve violent, brutal behavior are the result.

This latter category is the one that I see so often in my work as a psychologist among the inmates at the Southern State Correctional Facility, a state prison. The abused child becomes the abusive adult. Thus, breaking that chain by preventing child abuse — so horrible in itself — is surely a worthy goal.

Many in both the public and private sectors struggle with the complex problem of abused and neglected children, but solutions are elusive. The Division of Youth and Family Services is one agency that seeks to protect these children, and it was a year ago at a Division-sponsored conference on child abuse prevention that I first met Harry Gaynor. I was impressed by his commitment to his work in the field of child abuse by burning and interested in his discussion on the use of forensics to determine if a child's injury is accidental or intentional. He seemed to be a man with a mission. We talked and exchanged business cards, but I didn't expect our relationship to extend past an acquaintance.

However, two months later Harry called and described to me Charles Rothenberg's crime and his on-going correspondence with Charles. He asked if I would look over these letters from the professional viewpoint of a psychologist who works daily with men who have committed violent crimes.

The large packet of letters arrived, and I started reading. The letters painted a picture of a person who would hardly seem capable of such a terrible crime. They communicated rather a gentle, harmless, caring person. Yet I knew what he had done. Charles seemed to be separating himself from his past behavior and looking for someone to attach himself to.

New letters kept coming, and soon I agreed to co-author a book that would attempt to examine the evidence of Charles Rothenberg and to draw from that evidence conclusions that might point the way to preventing for others the abuse his son suffered.

The project was fascinating to me, particularly because Charles seemed such a paradox. I was eager to read his manuscript, but most of all I wanted to meet this man, to talk to him in person and to conduct some psychological tests. He obviously had a severe psychological problem. What was it in his life that had caused him to commit such a brutal act of violence?

Despite my enthusiasm, I knew I faced some difficult problems. I could perform only a superficial analysis through Charles' writing. I would be able to interview him, but that interview could never replace a longstanding therapeutic relationship. Testing would of necessity be brief and perhaps inconclusive. Thus, it was possible that my evaluation of Charles would be incomplete, or even flawed.

Nonetheless, I was determined to go ahead, to look for a pattern in Charles' development that could serve as a model to aid others, to help potential child abusers to think before they act. ■

Charles Rothenberg
The Early Years

I

My family is pretty much a mystery to me. I've met only a few of them and know very little about them — even my mother. It's hard to piece together my background because so much information is missing.

I do know that my mother, Clara Aza, was born in 1913 in the Ukraine, in Russia, and at the age of eight she, along with her brothers, Sam, Saul, Morris, and Isaac, immigrated to the United States under the name of Rothenberg.

How they left Russia, why they changed their name, and who helped them puzzle me to this day. Did they have relatives here? Where did they live? How were they educated? These questions have no answers for me. One fact: they all became U.S. citizens in 1940.

Mom was exceedingly beautiful and very intelligent. She spoke and understood at least eight languages, and she had a natural gift for music. She claimed she was in show business — a gypsy dancer. I saw a few photographs of her in costume, but I always had serious doubts about her profession.

I once saw Mom perform in a New Jersey nightclub, and it was just terrible! She couldn't dance or sing but managed to pull off her act with the gypsy costume, her fabulous appearance, and her smooth movements. The pity of it was that Mom thought she was terrific. I tried, but failed, to find out how Mom actually made a living over the years — how she paid her rent, bought food and clothes. If I asked, I was ignored.

I never met my father. I was illegitimate. Sam, my uncle, told me that Dad was a doctor and a good man. Mom told me the same thing. My birth certificate said that Dad was a bricklayer, born in Italy. This, of course, made me half Russian and half Italian. According to my birth certificate, my father's name was Charles Bocca.

My personal opinion is that what Mom and my uncles told me was false. I believe they wanted me to feel good and made up their stories, although I cannot be perfectly certain.

I was given the names Charles Aza, Charles Bocca, and Charles David Rothenberg. Because I was born out of wedlock, I always assumed the family gave me their last name (Rothenberg) after Mom died in 1960. I believe Mom decided to name me Aza, her maiden name, to hide a lot from me.

Saul, Sam, and Morris went to Harvard University and became pharmacists. They owned and operated their own drug stores near each other in Massachusetts — Boston, Cambridge, and Arlington. Sam owned five of them all over the state. Isaac was a window washer. All my uncles were of the Jewish faith. Sam was Orthodox and observed. They were good and kind men, hard-working and family-oriented.

Saul was married twice (both wives died of cancer), and he had two children. I met Morris only once, and I never met Isaac. Sam was married for 48 years, though he never had children, and he lived to be 92. I never really kept up with my uncles, except Saul. Saul told me I had another uncle, a dentist in the Bronx. I finally met him with Saul, but I never saw him again. His name was Arnow.

I had no close family ties with my mother or her relatives. I wished I did, though.

On June 20, 1940, I was born at Unity Hospital in Brooklyn, New York. Eleven days after my birth, I was placed in an orphanage somewhere in Brooklyn. I remained there until I was about five.

Then I was transferred to another orphanage, the Woodycrest Home in the Bronx. It was run by a women's organization in conjunction with the Department of Social Services of the City of New York — 100 boys and girls in all. I remained at Woodycrest Home until the age of 15 and was extremely fortunate to have been chosen and placed there.

Woodycrest Home was a nondenominational orphanage. The children either had no families, or came from families with serious domestic problems, or their parents just walked out on them. In my particular case, Mom was financially able to take care of me but thought it would be better and easier for her to keep me in a home.

We all had house parents in charge of us day and night wherever we went at the home and many places outside. I moved into different dormitories with new house parents as I got older. The dormitories usually had a minimum of 20 kids — a real homelike atmosphere. The girls, 25 to 30 in all, had two dormitories of their own. Woodycrest Home kept children only until they hit the age of 18. Then it was mandatory to leave. Many left before, for different reasons.

Those who had parents (and whose parents cared) went home on weekends and holidays. Those who were not as fortunate stayed behind but were treated very well. Activities were planned at the home, or we would go to movies or somewhere else. The home did not let me or the other kids feel left out.

Our weekly allowance was 50 cents. If we went to outside events, the home always paid for them. The other children and I were always treated with love and respect. They hired only house parents who cared!

Christmas was a fun time. I was fortunate, although this may sound strange, not to go with my mother — I never wanted to. We all wrote down three items we wanted from Santa Claus. When Christmas Day came, we went to the auditorium and were called up by Santa to receive our gifts. Then the director said a prayer, and we sang Christmas carols. As we marched out of the auditorium, we each received a stocking full of goodies. Of course, we had a Christmas tree, which we all helped dress up. My gift was always a basketball. It was all I wanted. I even slept with it.

We celebrated all the other holidays as well.

The home assigned me to a church called the Chapel of the Intercession, an Episcopal church on 155th Street and Broadway in Manhattan. Religious instruction was mandatory, and I went to church and Sunday School classes. Activities offered by the church were encouraged. I did participate, especially on Christmas, being the innkeeper's son in the Christmas pageant. How I loved it. I also enjoyed singing in the choir and playing on the church basketball team.

Thomas Woods, the custodian of the church and my basketball coach, became a close friend. He had a lovely wife, a daughter, and a son who was also named Tom. On many occasions, they invited me to their home, which was right on the grounds of the church. Sometimes when I had personal problems, I stayed with the pastor, Rev. Jennings, who also lived on the grounds.

There were two different directors while I was at the home, Mrs. Eleanor Parks and Dr. Douglas Merrill. They lived in an apartment right in the orphanage. My social worker's name was Miss Lois Wiley — a wonderful lady. How she helped me when I needed it and just wanted to talk ... about anything. She was a deeply caring and concerned individual.

My first childhood memory is of walking on white pebbles in a line with other children at a summer camp in Spring Valley, New York. I must have been around seven years old. As I walked up the hill to the camp to go to my quarters, I remember going over to a piano and starting to play, just banging on it. I was suddenly called to go down to a shed where my mother was waiting to visit me for the first time ever. Yet for some strange reason, I knew exactly what Mom looked like. There she was sitting on a bench. From that moment, I just do not remember the rest of the day.

Summer camp was really nice. Every year the orphanage sent me to Woodycrest Camp at Bear Mountain, New York, for two months. We all went together on a bus — an exciting time! The home even bought us whatever summer clothes we needed.

Summer camp is an experience everyone should have. Many children who live at home with their parents do not experience this joy. I was so fortunate, so very grateful! We all were.

We lived in wooden cottages and were taught to make our beds and clean the cottage every day. We had inspections each morning followed by the flag raising and breakfast. Then the fun began! So

24

many activities filled the day — swimming, hiking, baseball, basketball, rowing, and canoeing. I even learned how to "shake out" a canoe if it turned over and how to save lives with this technique. On rainy days indoor activities, such as movies, ping pong, pool, and cards, were planned. Once a week at a special canteen we could buy candy, cookies, gum, and other treats. Toothpaste, soap, and other necessities were given out at the cottages.

Once, my friend Kevin and I wandered off from a hike and got lost in the woods. We were really scared, especially when we saw a rattlesnake. When we heard the noise of cars, we followed the sound and walked along the highway until a police car picked us up and drove us back to camp.

At the end of the summer the camp director gave a party for all the children and handed out special awards. Some campers received trophies, some medals, some certificates — no one was left out.

Parents were invited to attend the party. A few came, but Mom never did. She visited me once at camp, but she made me feel uncomfortable by not participating with me in the planned events and by always drawing the attention to herself. She was probably very insecure, or maybe just self-centered. Who knows?

Henry Keiffer was my best buddy at the home. I called him "Buddy." He taught me a great deal about so many things, especially basketball. I wanted to be a professional basketball player then and hoped I would grow to be a seven-footer. Buddy and I always played together on the same teams at the home, at church, and at camp. He showed me all the tricks of the game — various shots, team effort, and good sportsmanship.

One day at the church (I was about thirteen), I was playing in a tournament against another church team. I was dribbling down the court when suddenly from behind the ball was taken out of my hand. I dropped to the floor in great pain with a badly sprained right arm. I couldn't play for a long time afterwards. For a year the pain kept coming back, especially when I would shoot a basketball or throw a baseball. It became so severe that I had to go to the hospital for new x-rays.

The doctors found a tumor on the upper part of the bone in my right arm close to the shoulder, and after many tests, I had surgery to remove it. Fortunately, it was not a cancerous growth, but I was in tremendous pain for months as they had scraped the bone to make sure the entire tumor was removed. Shortly after my discharge, I was readmitted to the hospital for a serious bone infection. It took me a year and a half to use my arm again. Mom came only once to see me while I was in the hospital. My house parents from the orphanage came twice a week.

II

Woodycrest was so good to me, much better than living with Mom. I really felt it was my home. I never missed having a family, since they treated me and all of the other kids so well.

The home had a television room, indoor swimming pool, gymnasium, a beautiful dining room, and a courtyard where we played and met our friends from the other dormitories. They arranged all kinds of activities for us, such as dances every Saturday evening, baseball games at Yankee Stadium and the Polo Grounds, and trips to the circus at Madison Square Garden, the rodeo, the Bronx Zoo, museums, movies, and the park. You name it, we had it — and extras, too!

We were treated like normal kids and learned about respect and manners, both to ourselves and others. When we misbehaved, we were punished by working in the kitchen or the dorm, missing a movie, or staying in for a weekend. If we disobeyed our house parents, we would get a ruler over our butts or the palms of our hands. Physical abuse was never used.

I always had a great love for animals. I wanted a dog, but we couldn't have pets at the home. Someone wanted to give a rabbit away, but I had nowhere to keep it, no cage or money to buy food. A man who sold fruits and vegetables at a stand I passed on my way to school gave me a cage and lots of food. So I took the rabbit and kept it in the bathroom. I used to run home from school every day to see it and worried about its safety.

One night a tiny kitten found its way into my room. How I loved it! I tucked it under my covers and went to sleep. The next morning the house parents saw it and found out I had a rabbit as well. Both had to go. I was very upset, but the house parents were nice enough to find a home for my pets.

There were times when I wanted to be with Mom. Sometimes I would not see her for weeks, months, or even years. Where she was, what she was doing, how she was making a living, why she never wrote me a letter, I never knew. When she did come to see me, I went with her in her big car that always broke down.

It was very boring staying with Mom. She never gave me affection, took me places, or even sat down and chatted like a friend. She never displayed her love for me. Mom would seldom talk to me about my Dad, and when she did, I think she lied. It wasn't the way she said things; it was her eyes that really told the story. Mostly Mom told me, "Dad was a good man, but he is dead," though if I asked to visit his grave, she ignored me. I never found out whether Dad was alive or dead, but I wanted to see him if I could. I didn't care about being born out of wedlock. It never bothered me because of my fine upbringing by the home. Whoever he was, wherever he may have been, or whatever he had done, he was still my Dad.

Mom married a doctor after I was born, but I never met him and never knew if he was my father. Mom divorced this man, and one of my uncles told me that he was not my real father. I do not even know if I ever had any brothers or sisters. It would have been nice to have a brother or a sister.

My first love at Woodycrest was Elizabeth Romirez. We were both shy, and, like most children, we had an on-again-off-again relationship. At camp we had a fight that the house parents broke up, and we were both punished. I was sent back to the home for three weeks, and Liz stayed at the camp with extra duties. She even wrote me a letter while I was away, and when I returned, we kissed and made up.

Returning to the orphanage after camp was really exciting for me, as I got ready to go back to school, met the new children coming into the home, and said good-bye to those who were leaving. Many who left were my dear friends. I used to cry a lot.

Before school started, we could have a week's vacation with our parents. Even if Mom would have shown up or wanted me, I always preferred to stay behind. I was uncomfortable with her and felt unloved and uncared for. Sometimes Mom left me at her apartment with no food and no money to buy any. Once I just went back to the home.

I went to elementary school at PS-73 in the Bronx, within walking distance of the home, and the years I was allowed to remain there were good. My teacher's name was Miss Cherrio, a tough cookie but an excellent teacher. The Department of Education assigned Mrs. Green, also a teacher at PS-73, to hold classes at the home. She was such a nice lady! I was taken out of PS-73 and enrolled in her class. Mrs. Green invited me to her home in Manhattan on a number of occasions. She taught me how to make a cake and allowed me to take it back to the home to share with my friends. All the years of my elementary education were a lot of fun!

When we graduated, Nancy Summer asked me to take her to the prom. She was also from the home and was built like a weightlifter; she had muscles and a body like a man. I knew in my heart that the others didn't really accept her because of the way she looked, but she was a kind, emotional, and sensitive person. I saw beyond her exterior. So we graduated together, went to the prom, and had lots of fun. I got hell for it from the other children who teased me, but I was always my own decision-maker and accepted the consequences of my own actions.

In September 1954 I entered Taft High School in the Bronx. I was eager to start on my studies and to make new friends. I also wanted to try out for the basketball team. I had two free passes, one for school lunches and the other for the New York City transit system. The home took me out to buy new school clothes, shoes, and sneakers. If I needed extras during the year, I received them — books, paper, pencils, and athletic clothes were all supplied. It was great!

Almost immediately, I met a new friend, Timmy Wrangler. Timmy lived in the heart of the slums and was not too bright, but he was warm and friendly. He was also very close to his family. Timmy was a real comedian with a personality like Richard Pryor or Don Rickles; every word out of his mouth was as funny as hell. He sure kept me in a laughing mood. I helped Timmy with his school work and even cheated for him so he wouldn't get bad marks and be demoted. We spent a lot of time together, riding bicycles, hanging out in the park, and even playing hooky. When his parents invited me for meals, I felt very comfortable. What I liked best was that they never spoke about the home and treated me just like a normal kid. I was!

The 15 years I remained at the orphanages did not make me a hard person. In fact, for some reason it made me very sensitive to the needs of others. I applauded those who had a normal family life, but I sometimes had problems when people asked, "Do you have a family?" Though I never showed it, it bothered me a great deal, and I tried to block it from my mind. I loved the Woodycrest Home, and it will remain with me forever. Some children who live with their families don't get the attention and love that I did.

Reflecting on my orphanage years, I was happy and never deprived of a normal, loving upbringing. I was taught to give for Him and to others; to love Him and others; to be obedient to Him and to others; to pray to Him and for others; to be kind, share, and forgive.

One day my social worker, Miss Wiley, called me into her office to tell me I would soon be released to my mother. I wasn't expecting this news and didn't know whether to be happy or sad. Then I began to cry and told her that I didn't want to leave. Woodycrest was so wonderful to me. I would be leaving my home and all my friends, too. Miss Wiley told me that my mother wanted to take me. She said that my departure would open up a space for another child who would then have the same opportunity I had had. Miss Wiley was right. I was happy that she cared about others, and I surely felt better hearing it. But I think Miss Wiley was concerned that things might not work out when I was released. She seemed to know that I would not be happy with Mom.

Two of my uncles, Sam and Saul, contacted Mom to ask if they could take me instead. Their plan was to enroll me into Worcester Academy, a military school in Worcester, Massachusetts, and then to send me to Harvard University to study to be a doctor. They wanted me to become something in life and to give me what Mom was not able to afford — an education. Love, too!

What I didn't know until later was that Sam and Saul also wanted me to be brought up in the Jewish faith. Since I was only a young boy, I didn't understand all of this, but I felt closer to God where I'd been taught over the years — the orphanage and the Chapel of the Intercession.

Nonetheless, Mom refused, and I could not go with my uncles.

For years, Sam sent Mom $75 a month that she was supposed to turn over to the home to help me out. When he suspected something was wrong, he investigated and found that Mom was spending the money on herself. He disowned his sister and didn't speak to her for a long time.

In October 1955 the sad day came when I had to pack and say good-bye to my friends, the house parents, and the staff. They even gave a party for me. Then I walked out the front entrance, got into a yellow cab with Mom, and drove away. ■

Charles Rothenberg
Transition

I

We drove to Manhattan. The taxi pulled up to the Hotel Aberdeen, a seedy-looking building with a dirty, torn canopy at the front entrance on 31st Street between Fifth and Sixth Avenues.

"Why are we stopping here?" I asked.

Mom replied, "This is where I live, son."

We went inside, and Mom introduced me to the manager. He, too, was dirty. The lobby was full of people, some of them nodding their heads and acting like alcoholics and drug addicts. I felt very uneasy. We rode the elevator to the third floor and entered Mom's apartment.

The apartment, which had two small rooms and one tiny bathroom, smelled musty and smoky. Then I heard a man's voice call out, "Is that you, Clara?" I waited in Mom's room, and she returned with Richard Stanawsky. She introduced us, but he left immediately. He had no manners at all. Mom told me that he was a very dear friend and he was sharing the apartment with us.

I looked around and went into Richard's room, which held two beds, a dresser, a table, and a loud clock. Richard was lying on a bed, listening to his radio and smoking up a storm in the dark room. Beer was on the table. I said hello, but he looked drunk and didn't say anything.

In Mom's room were a bed, a small electric stove, and a refrigerator. Trunks covered with thin, white paper stood in the center, and the room smelled of moth balls. It looked as if she had been away for a while and was just returning. Mom said I would be sleeping in her room. I knew that meant she was going to sleep in the other one.

When Richard left for his job as cook at the Belmont Cafeteria, I asked Mom all sorts of questions about him, why she was living with him and whether she was working. She told me to mind my own business.

I was very tired and hungry. Mom gave me a cup of soup, some bread, and a glass of milk, and then I went to bed. During the night I got up but could find neither Mom nor Richard. Much later, Richard came in drunk and made a lot of noise before falling on his bed. Soon after, Mom returned and they started arguing about money and why the rent hadn't been paid on time. I had a hard time sleeping that night.

Three days passed. I scarcely went out and had no proper meals. Mom and Richard were never home. I was so lonely — all the people I cared about were at Woodycrest. I went down to the dirty hotel lobby around 2:00 a.m. and sat alone and cried until Joe Maguire, the desk clerk, befriended me. He took me out for a meal, and he told me that Mom and Richard were going to be evicted for not paying their rent. I knew I would be okay because I could get help from the church. Joe gave me $5. I didn't believe his kindness and concern, but I liked it.

I had a habit of saying the Lord's Prayer when I was in need and feeling low. As Joe and I walked back to the hotel, I muttered the prayer to myself. I used to sing it at church in the choir.

Mom was waiting for me as we approached the hotel entrance. Maybe she was worried because she hadn't found me upstairs. But she was in a hurry and went out again. I knew I would have to leave Mom and her life-style.

I decided to follow her. Just by luck, I found her walking up Fifth Avenue. I wanted to know why she was out so much and what she was doing. Something was wrong, and ever since I entered that dirty hotel, I had a terrible feeling that Mom was not exactly doing the proper thing.

I followed her a long way, up to 72nd Street and Broadway. How the hell she walked this far was beyond me, but it made me very tired. It was already time for people to wake up and go to work. For quite a while, Mom walked up and down the street, sometimes standing and talking to different men. It was cold, and I didn't have the proper clothes. Finally, she started to walk with a man whom I thought she had been waiting for. How naive I was! I followed them to a run-down hotel-like building. Now I was shaking all over.

I waited for about ten minutes, hoping Mom would come out. Then I went in the building, and a man behind a glass enclosure immediately stopped me.

Speaking into some small holes in the glass, I asked, "Who was the couple who just came in?"

"Are you a cop?"

"No," I answered, "I know the lady."

"This place is for the johns that come in, a place for them to have fun."

I asked what johns were, and he thought I was kidding and called me stupid. Then he said, "They came in to have sex. The guy always pays the lady, and we get a percentage plus rent for the room. That lady you know is a regular customer."

I started to cry and ran out of that place. Very angry, I walked — ran — back to the Aberdeen Hotel. I related my experience to Joe and asked him if I could use the phone.

I called Tom at the church and told him what I had been through. I wanted to leave Mom right away, but I had no money and no place to stay. Tom told me to pack up and take a cab to his house. He'd pay for it, and I could stay with him until things were worked out.

I arrived exhausted. Tom put me to bed immediately, and I slept all day. I got up long enough to have dinner with Tom and his family, and went back to bed again.

We all went to church the next morning, and then Tom and Rev. Jennings wanted to hear my story from start to finish. It was painful, but I got through it. They agreed that I had to get out of Mom's environment immediately, but because I was a minor, there was a problem. I asked Rev. Jennings to call my Uncle Saul at his drug store in Arlington, Massachusetts, to see if he would consider taking me.

I was in luck! I was crying and very scared as Saul talked to me on the phone. It was decided — Rev. Jennings would give me the money to take a train to Boston where Saul would be waiting for me.

Rev. Jennings called Mom at the hotel. Mom was mad, I could tell, as Rev. Jennings gave it to her verbally. But he persuaded her that it would be in my best interest to be with Uncle Saul, and finally she agreed that I could go, at least for a while.

The next day Tom put me on a train at Pennsylvania Station. I knew as I rode those four hours that my life was not in order, but for some reason beyond my comprehension, I was a grown man at such a tender age.

When I arrived at South Station in Boston, Saul was right there waiting for me and told me that everything would be okay. He took me to the Kirkland Inn in Cambridge, just a few blocks from Harvard University and a couple of miles from his drug store, where I would have a room. The innkeepers gave me a warm welcome and a good meal, then showed me my room. It had a television in it! Boy, was I pleased! They fed me breakfast and dinner each day, and I ate lunch with Saul. He paid for everything, and extras. He gave me money and sent me to a nearby store to purchase some necessary clothing, which the clerk charged to Saul.

I rode on the bus to Belmont to meet Saul's family and have dinner with them. His wife, Ida, was a real tough lady who had no warmth — not even for Saul or her children. Saul introduced me to his children. Boy, did we get along!

Saul told me to report to work at his store and he would teach me how to make ice cream sodas. I came in every day from noon until closing at 9:00 p.m. I never got paid, but I was so very grateful. I was independent, had a place to live and food in my stomach, and felt at ease with no pressures.

On Sunday mornings I went to a nearby church with the owners of the Inn and attended a Bible study class. On Tuesday evenings I went to choir practice and sometimes sang on Sunday. Saul would let me off early on Tuesday evenings, though I didn't tell him why I wanted to leave before my usual quitting time. He didn't approve of my going to church, even when I was at the home, but I had no intentions of changing my life-style in this area. I loved the way I was brought up and the beliefs I was taught. Most of the time, I wanted to participate in services with the innkeepers. I enjoyed their company and friendship.

Mom called one afternoon at work. She pleaded with me to come to New York City to live with her. Although I loved Mom, I was happy and contented with Saul. After I hung up, Saul told me that his hands were tied. Mom was my legal guardian, and if I didn't return when she insisted, she could cause problems for him.

Saul was a compassionate man. He put his arms around me and said, "I will go back with you to New York and will try to have you come back here in a short time. But I cannot promise anything because of your mother."

I understood, but it was confusing. How would my life change again? It wan't normal, putting me on trains and throwing me around like a baseball.

Saul and I rode the train back to New York together, but he had to return to Massachusetts immediately. We hugged and kissed and said good-bye — and I was off with Mom to her new hotel, the Seville on East 29th Street.

We were met there by a Family Court investigator who said that because Mom couldn't take care of me at present, it was in my best interest to be put in a reform school. "You are not a problem child," he said," but you are too young to be on your own, according to state law. Until you're eighteen or your mother decides to take you back and can show the court she is able to do so, my hands are tied."

Mom tried to console me by making up stories, but I knew she manipulated my uncle to return me for the worse. Saul was unaware, for if he knew, he might have tried legally to keep me in Massachusetts.

The investigator took me to a boys' shelter in lower Manhattan. I did not like it there. Most of the boys were in for crimes; very few, like myself, were simply having family problems.

A social worker interviewed me for several hours and advised me that I would be going to Family Court in a few weeks. I was crying and very upset. She assured me that I was not the problem and that Mom just couldn't provide for me.

Mom didn't show up at Family Court, and the judge spoke to me in his chambers. He was really nice and gave it to me straight without pulling any punches. He committed me to Otisville State Training School for Boys in Otisville, New York. "You are being placed, not for misbehavior, but for problems your mother has caused you," he said. "These problems are not your fault, but I am obligated under the law to confine you until a suitable family setting can be arranged."

A few days later I was on my way upstate. At Otisville I was assigned to a cottage with a house parent in charge. We marched to meals every day, went to school and church, had recreational activities, and were responsible for certain chores. On many occasions, local basketball teams came in to play with us, which I enjoyed very much. But with all of this, I was not happy. I didn't belong here. I had to escape.

One afternoon I wandered off, hitched a ride, and returned to Manhattan. With no money and only the clothes on my back, I went directly to Rev. Jennings at the Episcopal church. He welcomed me with open arms, and we talked for a long time. I wanted to be independent, go to work, and pay my own share in life. Rev. Jennings reminded me that I could very well be picked up again by the juvenile authorities, but he agreed to sponsor me. "Don't worry," he said. "I will help you now and God will, too." He was a nice man!

The next morning I woke up very ill and was rushed to St. Luke's Hospital. The doctor advised me that I was in a serious run-down condition due to stress, and he prescribed rest. I remained at St. Luke's for three days, then returned to the church. For a month afterwards, I stayed with Rev. Jennings and worked with Tom at the church. I felt really good about putting in a full day's work, and I followed Tom's orders.

Rev. Jennings gave me a letter of recommendation to live at the Salvation Army's men's shelter in the Bowery where all the bums lived. The weekly rent was only $5.25, and the church would pay for it until I could find a job. Lining up with all the other men there, I would receive my food from the Salvation Army. Rev. Jennings gave me a weekly allowance so that I could use the city transit system and look for a job. In the meantime I continued to assist Tom.

I finally found my first job with Nina Products on West 18th Street. It was temporary, but I was making $40 a week. On weekends I would go to the owner's home on Long Island and mow the lawns, water plants, and clean his house. The extra 50 cents an hour really helped. It was off the books, too.

After six months, the company went bankrupt. Fortunately, I had managed to save money. I was still living at the shelter and economized by eating cheaply and getting my haircuts for 25 cents in the slums. For a long time I had nothing to do and little money, but next door to the shelter was a little church where services and activities kept me occupied. Many times I would take long walks and think a lot. I was lonely.

I had another long talk with Rev. Jennings and Tom. I also gave back some of the money they helped me with. I wanted to get out of the city and work around people, perhaps as a busboy or a waiter. Rev. Jennings called the personnel office at Grossinger's Resort in Liberty, New York, and eventually spoke with Jenny Grossinger herself. After hearing my story, she guaranteed me a job and a place to live. She even sent a check for $100 for work clothes and bus fare. This was unreal — a miracle! I mean, I didn't even know this lady. Rev. Jennings, Tom, and I went to the chapel and prayed together, giving thanks to God and to Mrs. Grossinger.

Tom was concerned about my inexperience and wanted to help me prepare for my new job, so he made me practice by working at church lunches. I learned fast and became a professional, at least at the church lunches.

I still had to go to Family Court. I was scared, but Rev. Jennings assured me that everything was going to be all right. When Mom entered the courtroom, I gave her a hug and a kiss, but she said very little. After the judge called my case, we went to his chambers. He got right down to business and didn't mince words. He reminded Mom that she had neglected me since birth and had not met her moral and legal obligations. The judge scolded her, and when she started to talk, he dismissed her from his chambers. I felt bad for Mom because of the way the judge treated her, but he was right.

Next the judge spoke directly to me: "You are hereby released in the custody of the church, under the direction of Rev. Jennings. You can now go to work anywhere you wish. You have come through a trying time, son, and I urge you to stay strong and keep in touch with Rev. Jennings."

I thanked the judge and rushed out of the courtroom to see Mom. I gave her a kiss and told her I would send her money. She didn't ever seem to be affectionate, but I loved her anyway, regardless of the past. It wasn't important now.

II

Soon I was ready to leave for the mountains. With tears streaming down my face, I hugged Rev. Jennings and Tom and boarded the bus for New York State. When I arrived, Paul Grossinger, the son of the owner, and Bill Maven, the maître d', talked with me and outlined my responsibilities. Starting as a busboy, I would train for a week to learn the kitchen and dining area. Mr. Grossinger instructed Mr. Maven to help me as much as possible to learn the business. I expressed my gratitude for this opportunity and offered to work every day. They thought I had a great attitude and looked like a hard worker.

I learned fast. Before you knew it, I was a waiter and was making the real bucks. It was hard work with 12- to 14-hour days the norm. I was 17, able to send Mom a weekly money order and to repay the church for what they had done for me, and much more. I kept in touch with Rev. Jennings and Tom. If it got slow at Grossinger's, I would go down the road and work at the Concord Resort in Monticello, just to keep busy. Reliability was essential in my line of work, and word got around that I was always available. The hotels in the mountains had a problem employing good workers.

The time sped by, and I enjoyed being around and talking to my customers. I loved children and would even babysit. My social life, however, was not that great. I was shy and backed off asking for dates. Sometimes I would go out with a customer, but I was kind of choosy. I was always lonely. Making money was not enough, and something was missing that I couldn't pinpoint. Sometimes after work I would go to the movies or just walk into a nearby church and say a few prayers. I had no friends and felt like a workaholic with no purpose, no goals.

A year passed, and I was still lonely, despite brief visits to New York when I would say hello to Mom and stop by the church. I had saved a lot of money and finally made up my mind to return to New York. I gave my notice to Mr. Maven and saw Paul and Jenny Grossinger to tell them how grateful I was for their help. I gave Jenny an envelope containing $100 to repay what she had sent to Rev. Jennings for me so many months ago. She started to cry and returned the envelope to me, saying I should keep the money or use it to help someone else. Jenny and Paul told me I could come back to Grossinger's anytime I wanted.

When I arrived in New York, I went directly to the church. The first thing I did was to give the $100 to Rev. Jennings to assist someone in need. I'm sure Rev. Jennings used it well. At least I knew wherever it went, it would help someone.

Tom got me a room with a nice family on 158th Street, three blocks from the church and for only $8 a week. I rejoined the choir and the basketball team and found a job in a night club at the Empire State Building working only five days a week. I was very happy. I was making decent money, and I now had the chance to be with friends at the church and maybe to find other interests as well.

III

I met a nice girl — Anita Sanchez from Puerto Rico. Her family was poor and lived only a few blocks from my room; I got very close to them. Anita and I were going steady and went to church together. Her mother, Pilar, and her sister, Alma, went to a nearby Roman Catholic church. Sometimes I went to their services as well and even learned two Latin Ave Marias. After church services I always took them out for lunch and sometimes to a movie.

Another year went by, and my life was happy. I never felt the pressures, worrying about myself all the time. I was close to the church, Anita, and her family, and I had a good job. Things were just perfect!

One day Anita unhappily told me that she and her family had to return to Puerto Rico in a few weeks. She wanted to complete her education, which was too expensive in New York, and they thought the opportunities were greater there. We spent that evening together, talking and sharing our thoughts. I assured her I would go to the airport with her, even if I was working. I would just call in sick. I also promised to write to her and visit her soon.

Anita and I corresponded for over a year. I was unable to go to Puerto Rico right away, what with changing jobs and my involvement with the church. I had also taken a second job as file clerk at New York University after Anita left.

But I grew lonely again, and I finally decided to go to Puerto Rico. Anita and her mother were so happy! Rev. Jennings and Tom thought it was a great idea, since they felt I worked too hard and could use the rest. I made arrangements to pay my rent a few weeks in advance and to mail my rent if I stayed longer. The elderly lady who owned the apartment belonged to the same church as I did. I helped her a lot.

It was October 31, 1960. I went to visit Mom at the Seville Hotel. Richard was there, drunk, and Mom came down to the lobby to see me. I told her I was going on vacation and would return before Christmas to spend time with her. I begged her to reconsider her life-style and offered to find an apartment where we could live together when I returned, but she didn't seem interested. I gave her some money, hugged and kissed her, and hopped into a cab. I remember looking out the back window. Mom was wearing black as she always did, and I kept my eye on her until she disappeared. When I arrived at the airport, and I had time to call Mom again. I told her I loved her and would be back soon.

I boarded the plane — my first flight — and was soon in San Juan being greeted by Anita and her family. We drove to their home in San Lorenzo, about two hours away, and arrived late at night. After having some coffee and hot bread, Anita took me to a small barn at the back of the house where a folding bed with a mosquito net over it was ready for me. Anita and I asked her mother's permission to take a walk. Before we left, I opened the refrigerator to get something to drink and was stunned to see it almost empty.

We walked to the town's plaza where we sat on a bench and talked for hours. Anita cried and poured out all the difficulties her family was having without enough money for food and clothes. Her mother's second husband was an alcoholic and beat her all the time. Anita seemed to be reaching out to me for help. I put my arms around her and said, "Everything will be okay, you'll see."

At last we walked back to the house, and I gave Anita $50. She didn't want to take it, but I forced it into her hand. We slept for a while, but I was awakened by a man screaming at the top of his lungs and beating Pilar. It went on for quite some time, and Anita and Alma came into the barn crying. They climbed into my bed; I covered them and slept beside them on the concrete floor. We were all afraid.

Later Pilar came out to the barn with a black eye. She was afraid to go back into the house, as her husband was still asleep, and she asked me to deal with him. I threatened to call the police to have him arrested for beating his wife if he didn't leave, so he gathered his belongings and went away. He was still drunk.

Anita gave Pilar the $50, and then we went to the supermarket. I told Pilar not to worry about money and to take the things she needed for a week. She was very shy about choosing items, so Anita and I went through the store and piled up the cart with everything imaginable.

Anita and I also made plans to fix up the house — paint, phone, and bathroom pipes. Pilar just stood by and watched. She was a strong, proud woman and felt comfortable with me around, being part of the family.

I finally decided to get a job and stay for a while. I had given them practically all my money, so I set out to find a waiter's position in San Juan. With no difficulty, I was hired by the El San Juan Hotel near the airport, and I worked in their Tropicana Night Club in the evenings, making excellent wages and tips. I travelled back and forth on public transportation — a two-hour trip — but it was worth it. I just loved Anita and this family.

Pilar's husband didn't seem to support or even care about his family. I wanted to help them get on their feet and live normal lives without fearing where the next meal would come from. I set up a bank account for them, which only Anita knew about, and she handled all my earnings.

Anita introduced me to her pastor, Father Michael Duffy. Apparently, she had told him a great deal about me and my decision to stay in Puerto Rico. Father Duffy and I became close friends and many times sat in his pastoral office and chatted about God, my life, prayer — you name it. He was a kind, warm, loving, and gracious man of God, and we hit it off from the very beginning. Sometimes Father Duffy and I would go into the hills together on my days off, and I would help him with services for the poor people living in huts along the dirt road. I was especially attached to one child who lived near me, and I always had a lollipop in my hand for her.

The weeks had gone by rapidly, but I began to miss Mom. With Christmas approaching, I wanted to spend the time with her and bring her a few gifts. But I knew it would be hard to break the news to Anita and her family.

I had saved a great deal of money to secure the family, and I gave Pilar the bank book that Anita had managed. They were receiving some food from the welfare commissary, and I gave Father Duffy some money to hold in case of emergency. I planned to send them a money order every week and to return one day.

I gave my notice at the hotel and spent the last week with Anita, much of the time with her family just going to various functions and having a lot of fun together. On Christmas Eve I was booked on a flight to New York. I said my good-byes to Father Duffy and the child I was so fond of. Father Duffy assured me that if anything came up, he would contact me. He knew I loved Anita and her family. He blessed me, and I assured him he would see me again.

The whole family sadly drove me to the airport. Pilar and Alma said good-bye with lots of hugs and kisses and left Anita and me alone. We both started to cry. There was nothing to say, and we embraced until the boarding announcement. I told Anita how much I loved her, and she said the same thing to me. As I was heading for the plane, I heard them all yelling at the tops of their lungs, "We love you, Charles! Come back, we love you!"

That last step I took onto the plane gave me a chill, and all of a sudden I was very lonely. My seat was near the front of the plane, and I kept waving until I couldn't see my friends any longer. My eyes were full of tears the whole way back, and I wrote letters to Anita and Father Duffy.

I arrived at LaGuardia Airport late that afternoon. Snow was falling, and the wind made it even colder. I had no overcoat, only a warm sweater. After I picked up my baggage, I went to a pay phone to call Mom.

When I asked to speak to Mom, the switchboard operator asked who I was. When I told her, she seemed nervous and questioned me about where I had been for the last two months. She said everyone had been trying to reach me. "Didn't you read the newspapers?" she asked.

I was really getting upset by all these questions. The manager got on the phone and advised me that something serious had occurred. When I asked him to put my mother on the phone, he said, "We've been trying to locate you since October 31st and so have the police. You've been in every newspaper in New York. You must come immediately to the hotel."

Finally, the owner came on the line. He said, "Charles, this is the owner of the Seville. I have some very bad news for you, son. On October 31st at midnight your mother was killed on 34th Street and Fifth Avenue."

I dropped the telephone and ran out of the phone booth, crying, "Oh my God, Mom is dead." ■

Charles Rothenberg
Living on the Edge

I

I kept running and crying and yelling that Mom was dead. I went into a rest room and poured cold water over my face, trying to look as normal as possible. My face was very red. Then I caught a cab back to the city.

In the cab I started to cry again and to think about how Mom was killed. It had occurred the same evening I had waved good-bye to her on the corner of 29th Street and Fifth Avenue. I remembered telling Mom how I wanted to get a new place for us and wondered what role Richard might have played in her death.

My thoughts were confused and raced from one thing to another. How I missed Anita in Puerto Rico! Bible passages came into my mind — lessons on forgiveness and the parable of the Good Samaritan. I was never an angry individual before — why now?

I suspected Richard. He drank a lot and was very rude to Mom. I didn't know the answers yet, but so many thoughts flooded my mind. After all, Mom was the only family I really had left. It hit me very hard to realize that I was alone now, 20 years old and out in the world working for five years. I knew things were going to change. It was a terrible feeling that I couldn't understand or shove aside.

The cab driver noticed how upset I was. He was consoling and considerate and didn't even charge me for the ride. I looked at him like he was crazy or kidding me, but he hadn't started the meter seeing my condition. Nonetheless, I dropped a ten dollar bill in the front seat, thanked him for his kindness, and ran into the Hotel Seville.

The desk clerk put his arm around my shoulders and led me into the manager's office. I started to cry again and asked a lot of questions. "Who killed Mom? Was it Richard? Why?"

Crying seemed to help me release the anger and hostility I had within me. I was desperate to find out what had happened.

The owner spoke to me kindly, "Charles, your mother was hit by a taxi on November 1st at midnight on the east corner of 34th Street and Fifth Avenue. She died eight hours later at Bellevue Hospital of extreme internal bleeding and multiple injuries. We had a terrible rain storm that night, and witnesses said that the taxi skidded on the wet pavement as your mother was crossing the street. She was dressed in black, and because of the heavy rain and wind, the driver did not see her until his headlights actually hit her. He immediately stopped and called for help.

"A police officer tried to get one of your mother's arms out from under the wheel, but he couldn't do it. The main artery was probably crushed under the wheel, so he waited for the ambulance. When it arrived, they backed up the cab to release your mother's arm, then took her to the hospital.

"She was in a coma until shortly before her death, when she awoke and asked for you. You were in all the newspapers for a week, but no one could locate you."

He showed me several newspaper articles, one with a picture of Mom lying in the street looking like she was reaching out for help from under the cab.

At first, I was confused. I still thought that Richard had killed her but was relieved after seeing the newspaper accounts. Richard still lived at the hotel, and I signed an authorization for the house detective go in and take Mom's personal belongings for me without having problems with Richard.

The owner was really nice. He offered me money and a room at the hotel without charge until I could get on my feet, but I refused both. He told me that Uncle Saul had been notified of my mother's death and that he had arranged for her burial the next day in New Jersey.

It was late by now, but more than anything I wanted to visit Mom's grave. The hotel owner let the desk clerk off early, and he drove me to the cemetery. With my thoughts swirling, I knelt by the grave for some time, praying for Mom's soul. I prayed that she hadn't felt any pain when she was struck and had died peacefully. This I'll never know.

The desk clerk drove me back to the hotel where I called Rev. Jennings. Within two hours, he and Tom picked me up. I could tell by their faces they knew what had happened. It was about 2:00 a.m., and I was very tired. The desk clerk invited us next door for breakfast, but I only wanted to leave the hotel.

I stayed with Rev. Jennings for three weeks and worked on the church grounds with Tom, hoping that work would help to release my anger and pain. I spent many hours talking to them and their families about my feelings and blowing out the steam I had in me. It made me feel better for the time, but I was still lonely.

I finally moved back to my old room and returned to my old job, working seven days a week. The long hours and being around people helped to push back the loneliness, but after work, it started all over again. I was too shy to go out and meet people, especially in New York. It was just hard, very hard, to be nice in this big city. I even took a second job because of my depression.

Six months passed. I wanted so much to go to Puerto Rico and ask Anita to marry me. We had been corresponding all this time, but I never brought up the subject of marriage. In June 1960 I talked it out with Rev. Jennings and Tom and decided to go to Puerto Rico. I was so lonely, and earning money was not enough. I wanted to make my own family, have kids, and live a normal life. They agreed that if Anita was the right woman and she felt the same way about me, this would be just the medicine for me.

I gave notice on my job and made arrangements with my landlord. Once again Rev. Jennings and Tom drove me to the airport. I wondered how things would be if I didn't have the wonderful friends I had met at the Chapel of the Intercession.

II

Anita was right there waiting for me at the San Juan Airport. How my heart bounded when we embraced! We spent most of that day in San Juan. Anita made me aware of the financial problems that were once more besetting them. Pilar had to use the money I left behind to get a divorce from her husband and to survive. I told Anita about my life since I left the island — how lonely and depressed I was and how I wanted again to help her and her family.

This time things were really bad for Anita. I had brought only $1,000 in cash with me, and I gave most of it to them. I went back to work at the night club in San Juan immediately before I could even spend time with Anita. But I was going to help them all, and I was content.

Because tourism was down and business was slow, the hotel industry was experiencing heavy layoffs, and I received my pink slip. The unions caused problems with picketing and violence at some hotels when nonunion workers attempted to cross the lines. I would have been seriously hurt if I tried to cross. For a while I picked sugar cane for $2 an hour without telling Anita or Pilar and tried unsuccessfully to get another job.

One day I was sitting with Anita in her friend's house, and suddenly I asked her to marry me. She look stunned! I was stunned, too! Although we were very close, we were both young, and I knew in my heart that I was proposing out of loneliness and desperation. Anita and I were mature, but we were not ready to get married. Anita said, "Not now. Let's wait until we're older and I complete college."

The money I gave to Anita and her family was dwindling fast. I wanted to help them, but I was out of work and didn't know what to do. Their situation was desperate. I thought hard about how I could get a quick buck and formulated a wild and crazy plan that I could pull off only with a lot of luck.

I got up early one morning, and, telling Anita I was looking for a job, went to San Juan. I walked into the Royal Bank of Canada, approached the area where American Express travelers checks could be purchased, and asked for $1,500 in travelers checks. The teller brought out a pouch full of checks and asked what denominations I wanted. I told her and kept talking, hoping she would be distracted and would leave the pouch on the counter. I deliberately changed my mind to confuse her after she asked me to fill out a form. She was called to the phone, and I saw my chance. I picked up the pouch, tucked it under my arm, and walked slowly out of the bank. I walked a few blocks, then hailed a cab to take me back to San Lorenzo. When I counted the travelers checks in the pouch, I discovered they were worth $4,300.

I was really nervous. I knew I had done something wrong and wondered if I'd get caught, but the only thing on my mind was to help Anita and her family so they could have regular meals and get back on their feet. I did not think about the ultimate consequences, but it didn't really matter. All I knew was that I had the money that this family needed.

I could never figure out why I always wanted to help people, and on many occasions I did it both honestly and dishonestly. I just felt good about it.

Nothing about my crime was in the newspapers or on the radio, and after a few days I started to feel comfortable spending the money. I cashed $1,000 of the checks at a Rio Piedras bank with my own name. I gave Anita and her mother the money and told them to pay their bills and fill up the ice box. I also purchased a used car for them.

Weeks passed, and there was still nothing about this bad thing I had done. Then one day I saw a headline on the front page of the newspaper: "Royal Bank of Canada Robbed of $4,300 in Travelers Checks." I was very nervous!

A few days later as I left the house to take a walk, I was arrested. The officers took me to the San Lorenzo Police Department for a few hours, then transported me to San Juan where I was lodged in the La Princesa county jail in Puerta de Tierra. All this time I was wondering, "What would Anita and her family be thinking? Would they be all right?" They had enough money, and I wasn't going to tell the authorities they had it. They needed it.

I was questioned the next morning and shown the photograph taken by the bank's hidden camera. Bail was set at $20,000, then reduced to $10,000. The investigator told me he had spoken to Anita and her mother, and I started to cry. Apparently, Pilar told the police that I stole the checks to help them and that they had spent all the money. I was glad because they needed it.

Sometime later, Father Duffy visited me and brought me a rosary and a letter from Anita. He said a few prayers, and we talked about why I had stolen to get Anita and her family out of poverty.

"I always want to help people and to do good to others," I said.

Father Duffy answered, "Charles, this was the wrong way to do it, and you will have to be punished." He told me to believe in God and pray.

I spent weeks in this dirty county jail, eating rice and beans at every meal and drinking coffee that tasted like mud. There were no toilets or showers. Fighting among the inmates was routine, along with homosexual activities committed either by free will or by force. I was on my hands and knees every day scrubbing floors. I received no letters from Anita and felt I had been forgotten until one day I was called out to be released on bail — a complete shock!

My heart was pounding as I was taken downstairs to the front entrance, where Anita and her mother and sister were waiting for me with open arms and lots of hugs and kisses. Pilar had put up her house to make my bail. I didn't know what to say, but I walked out of that hell hole and cried all the way back to San Lorenzo. They told me how much they loved me and that they wanted to help me. I vowed to go back to work right away and continue to help them, to show up in court on my scheduled days, and to do the right thing.

With the rainy season setting in, the tourist trade was still slow and finding work was difficult. Since my name had been in the newspapers, I was afraid that a prospective employer would recognize me.

I was still a lonely individual — from childhood — and always wanted to help people. Many of my decisions over the years were based on these feelings and on an impulse for others, not on thinking a situation through. My desire overcame reality, but when I did help someone else, it always made me feel good.

I asked Anita again to marry me, but she refused. She loved me like a brother, she said, but couldn't see any future for us beyond this relationship. She had a crush on a boy from a wealthy family. Although I was happy for her, I was deeply saddened and hurt — but I told Anita that I understood. To myself, I wondered if anything was wrong with me. I always had bad luck with women. All they would say is that I was a really nice guy, good-looking, and maybe too giving. Many called me a sucker because I was too caring or nice. I still had Mom on my mind and was confused and lonely with no direction or plan in life. I wanted one, though.

I went to court, but the case was postponed for four months. The judge granted my request to return to New York so I could go to work and make restitution for the money I had stolen.

Anita and her family took me to the airport for a big send-off. As I walked out to the plane, I turned around to wave good-bye. There they were on the upper platform screaming, "We love you, Charles. Write to us. Call us. We love you!" How I wanted to remain with them, and how lonely I would be in New York. I sat next to a window and watched until I couldn't see them any longer as the plane lifted into the sky.

III

It was mid-July when I returned to the hot, sticky city. I hopped a cab and went to my apartment. The landlord had passed away, and all of my belongings were gone. New residents had taken over the apartment, and no one helped me to locate my things. Fortunately, I was able to rent a room nearby. I had enough clothing to wear and money for a week, and I was off to look for a job. I found work seven days a week as well as a part-time job to make extra money to send to my friends in Puerto Rico. The rest I put in the bank. After a while, I managed to repay Pilar the money she had put up for my bail, plus a weekly money order of $80.

For seven weeks I worked hard, making money hand over fist, honestly, working around the clock. I again became extremely lonely and depressed over my mother's death. I felt I was living without a purpose, just surviving, without any friends. I wanted to stop working and make a fast buck to return to Puerto Rico for good. I didn't tell Rev. Jennings or Tom about what I had in mind, although we had long talks about my depression and continued loneliness. It was always there for some reason.

I purchased a broken 22-caliber gun — at least it looked real — and decided to hold up a clerk at Grand Central Station where he sold travelers checks and had lots of money behind his bullet-proof window. I approached the clerk late one night when no one was around, pointing the gun through the hole in his window and demanding that he hand over all the checks and money he had. He immediately ducked to the floor where I couldn't see him. I panicked and ran out of the station to the Roosevelt Hotel nearby. I was shaken up, hungry, and tired. I ate at an all-night coffee shop in the hotel, then sat down in the lobby where I fell asleep.

The hotel's security searched me as I slept, found the broken gun, and called the police. The clerk I had tried to rob identified me, and I was arrested for attempted robbery in the second degree. I was fingerprinted and taken off to The Tombs in lower Manhattan. I knew I might never see Anita and her family again.

I was housed with men who had committed all sorts of crimes, many of them violent. The atmosphere was terrible, and the officers treated us badly. There were food strikes, stabbings, and brutality. I had to watch my shadow. I stayed up night after night thinking about Anita and her family, praying to God they were all right. I didn't want them to know I was in trouble again, so I didn't write to them. I also knew that I had fled from my charges in Puerto Rico, and a warrant for my extradition could be lodged against me.

During the four months I spent at The Tombs, I saw my attorney, was interviewed by the Probation Department, and went back and forth to court. In December, sentencing day finally arrived. When asked by the judge to say something before sentencing, I only stated that I knew I had done wrong. My attorney spoke for a few minutes and read the recommendation for five years' probation from the report of the Probation Department. Nonetheless, the judge sentenced me to three to six years at Sing Sing in Ossining, New York.

I was aghast! I didn't know what was going to happen, but I didn't expect prison life. Here I was, 21 years old and scared to death, going to Sing Sing. What a terrible feeling!

I stayed at Sing Sing for 90 days for medical examinations, psychological evaluation, and classification and then was transferred to Greenhaven Prison in Stormville, New York.

Assigned to the kitchen to prepare the meals, I was disgusted by what went on there. Inmates put razor blades in the meat, urinated into the soup and gravy pots, and stirred glass into the mashed potatoes. It was such a sick situation that after a few weeks I just quit and refused to go back to work. I was locked up until I went before the Principal Keeper to plead my case, and he reassigned me to the education department to learn how to type. Within six months I could type 40 words per minute, and since my rapport with the teacher was excellent, he secured a full-time job for me with his supervisor, Mr. Harter.

A year passed, and I wanted to get as far away as possible from the other inmates who were manipulative, pushed drugs, made their own alcohol, and somehow procured weapons that led to gang violence in the yards. I requested a job change and was assigned to work in the mail room, right in the front office around the administration employees. There time went by much better for me in all areas.

My friend, Father Duffy, made a surprise visit one day. Boy, was I happy to see him! We talked for hours on either side of a wire barrier, mostly about Anita and her family. (He found out I was in prison because the authorities had contacted Pilar.) He said that they all sent their love and had never forgotten me.

Before Father Duffy left, he passed me a rosary through the wire screen. I wanted something of his to keep — to be part of him, the man I looked to as the father I never had. I just loved him — and still do. He prayed for me, and we promised to write to each other. He told me never to give up hope, that all I needed was to believe that God forgives me unconditionally.

Father Duffy and I corresponded for the rest of my stay at Greenhaven, and he kept me informed of Anita and her family. I didn't receive many letters while I was in prison, as I really had no one to write to. It was very lonely not hearing from anyone.

My first application for parole was denied because I had no place to go, no program set up or job offer. I thought the whole world had fallen in on me and got very nervous. I started to lose weight and was finally hospitalized with pneumonia. They must have thought I was going to die because I was in an oxygen tent for three days and a Roman Catholic priest was called. The priest came every day, said prayers for me to get better, and gave me a Bible. He told me I kept yelling, "Anita ... Father Duffy ..." Within a month I had regained my strength and went back to my wing and work in the mailroom.

I went to Catholic services every Sunday and to Bible studies. I wanted to join the prison choir, but most of the inmates did that only to show off and be recognized. My only concern was to pray and to listen to the sermon. Sometimes I assisted the priest with the services, which was meaningful to me.

In December, 1965, I was scheduled for another parole hearing. This time my pre-release program was all arranged with the help of the Salvation Army. I had a place to live and a job as a clerk typist for a Manhattan attorney, Benjamin Meyers. My counselor had also approved the plans.

The hearing went well, and I was given a date for my freedom. I was so happy I was just about jumping for joy. Now I would be able to start my life all over again.

IV

Three days before my scheduled release, however, my counselor informed me that a warrant had been received from the Commonwealth of Puerto Rico requesting my extradition for my 1960 crime. I had put that incident out of my mind, and now I was really shaken up. I had the option of fighting extradition proceedings, but I waived my rights and agreed to cooperate.

All my plans and hopes and dreams of starting a new life were gone. Again, I felt as if the whole world had fallen on top of me. I had only a few days left but decided not to tell any of the inmates about my problem, as rumors would spread and inmates seemed to enjoy harrassing others. I have always been too sensitive and emotional.

Two plainclothes officers picked me up at the prison. They advised me that they would not handcuff me because I was not considered dangerous, but if I attempted to run, I would be shot. We stopped for lunch on the way to the airport, and I even had the freedom to go to the bathroom by myself. Although carefully watched, I could have run; but I wanted to get this over with, do my time, and get on with my life. Once in Puerto Rico, I was handcuffed and taken back to La Princesa.

The conditions were even worse than before. The prison was overcrowded, and tension was running high between inmates and guards. The brutality was terrible as inmates were beaten with sticks or hosed down with torrents of water. Some were even killed.

After some days I had a visit from the attorney who had handled my case five years before. I recounted the brutality and told him I had been hosed down once for no reason when other imates were fighting. He spoke to the warden and warned him that he would take action immediately if I was harmed. The warden guaranteed my safety but claimed no brutality was occurring at the prison. My attorney advised me to plead guilty and throw myself on the mercy of the court.

Anita and Pilar surprised me with a visit one day. We were not allowed to touch each other, but they assured me how much they loved me. Pilar was working, and Anita was still in college. I apologized to them for running away and was relieved to hear that they had received all the money I sent. It was difficult to hold back our tears. We had only five minutes to talk, and it broke my heart to see them walk away and disappear around the corner.

As the weeks went by, tension mounted at the jail. Guards beat up on inmates, and inmates acted like animals, ready to retaliate at any moment. One night I awoke to find a group of inmates with weapons in their hands preparing to escape through a tunnel. But something went wrong. Shots rang out, and they all went to the roof for a confrontation that was to end with several inmates killed and many injured. I was forced to the roof with some other inmates who refused to participate, and the entire prison was surrounded by the National Guard with rifles pointed at us. An inmate who had been standing right next to me was killed when he tried to climb a fence.

The standoff continued for hours, and the inmates' demand to talk to the head of the Justice Department about prison conditions was refused. Suddenly helicopters landed on the roof and an attack force entered the prison, ending the siege as quickly as it began. We were all immediately searched, questioned, and transported to the State Penitentiary at Rio Piedras where we stayed in a holding tank for days with little food or water — a horrible experience.

My attorney obtained a court order to have me released from the tank and treated humanely. When I went to court, I pleaded guilty and received a sentence of one to two years. I returned to the prison and was assigned a job and a new dormitory.

There I was befriended by another inmate, Robert Manners, who took me under his wing. I slept on the upper level of his bunk in a congested and overcrowded tier. Most of the inmates were depraved, with abnormal sexual activities routine. I saw killings over gambling, homosexuality, food — you name it. The guards were violent and beat the prisoners. Medical treatment was rare unless someone was close to dying. I was fortunate to have a good friend, and I kept my mouth shut. I wanted to get through these two years unharmed.

Father Duffy wrote to me, but he was very busy with his people and serving God. He always told me never to give up hope. I had one visit from Pilar, who informed me that Anita had been in a coma for weeks after a terrible car accident. She had finally come out of it, but her life was still in danger.

Pilar put her arms around me and said, "We all love you, Charles. You are too good, and in your life you will get hurt over your giving and caring. People will step all over you and take advantage of you. You must learn to say no at times and not give so much."

I answered, "Some things in life we cannot change, Pilar. I have always been this way."

Because of Anita's critical condition, her doctor arranged for me to see her and to give blood for her. She had constantly called out my name, and he felt that a visit from me might help her turn the corner. Dressed in civilian clothes and without handcuffs, I was escorted to the hospital by two prison guards and my social worker.

The doctor said, "Anita needs to see you, and you must give her strength to live. Your presence is essential for her emotional health and will provide something the medical profession cannot."

Anita's entire head was bandaged. Other parts of her body were badly bruised and broken, and it had taken 75 stitches to sew her up. I went over to her bed, kissed her, and talked with her for a long time. She told me how she missed me and wanted me to be her brother forever. I replied that I would — and anything else she desired — as long as she got better. I had to complete my prison sentence, but I promised to write.

I poured out my feelings to her — how I loved her and would do anything for her. All she had to do was ask. She seemed contented, and perhaps my visit did help her. I remember saying, "You are the only girl I have ever loved."

Just before I left, my social worker came into the room and told us that my case would be submitted to the Parole Board for consideration of an early release for good behavior. We were surprised and very pleased about this wonderful, sudden news.

Afterwards, the doctor thanked me and added, "God bless you, Charles. This may have just done the trick."

A month later, I went before the Parole Board and gained my freedom without conditions. I had already received a one-way plane ticket from the Gordon family in New York. I had met this family when I got out of the orphanage, and they apparently had kept in touch with the Puerto Rican authorities on my situation.

I was now 25 years old, and I wanted to be baptized as a Roman Catholic. I felt very close to the church. A nun, Sister Emilia Rodriguez, befriended me in prison and gave me religious instruction. Father Duffy baptized me at St. Augustine's Church in San Juan in a short, private ceremony. He had been elected head of his order, the Redemptionist Fathers, and was to be transferred to New York.

V

It was the summer of 1965 when I was released. The Gordon family took me in when I arrived in New York. Kitty Gordon, the mother, had 18 children, eight of whom were living with her. She was divorced, and I understood that her ex-husband never helped to bring up the children. I helped her while living at her home.

I got a great job as a clerk typist at the Omega Lighting Company on Park Avenue with a lot of responsibility and long hours. At one point, a 13-day transit strike made it very difficult to get to work, but I didn't miss a day. I built up a lot of experience over two years and received regular raises and Christmas bonuses. Sometimes I went to church, but mostly I was working too many hours, plain lazy, or too tired. I did visit Rev. Jennings and Tom, though.

In the spring of 1967 I moved away from the neighborhood I had been living in, which was turning bad with drug addicts and crime and made me very uncomfortable. I rented a little room on Clinton Avenue in Brooklyn a few blocks away from Pratt Institute and St. Joseph's College. I kept in touch with Anita and her family all this time and sent them regular money orders, but my loneliness was still there. Something was always missing.

One day I received a letter from Anita. She wanted to come to New York! She had a place to live with a friend, which was quite near my rented room, and she needed me to send her the air fare. But the reason she wanted to leave Puerto Rico was that Victor, the boy she was in love with, had raped her in the back seat of his car. She had told no one else, and I was grateful she considered me her brother and trusted me. I called Anita that night and made the necessary arrangements. Her mother and sister also intended to live in New York, but they were making their own plans.

Several weeks later, Anita arrived. She came running to me, putting her arms around me and crying, but her eyes were radiant with happiness. Her roommate was away for the week, and I knew Anita had arranged this time to spend with me so we could be together.

That evening we talked and talked. Anita needed to get it all out of her system and made me promise not to tell her mother or Father Duffy. It seems that they had gone to a dance and Victor had gotten drunk. They were sitting in the back of his car, making out, when he grabbed her, held her mouth, and raped her. Then he passed out. She was too frightened to tell anyone and didn't want a scandal, but she knew that she could talk to me and I would understand. How I wanted to help her!

For hours, Anita just poured her heart out to me. We shared our thoughts and ideas, and I tried to come up with some solutions to help her cope with the problem and put her at ease. She seemed very much relieved. After all, she had belted out for the first time her feelings about this terrible tragedy, her anger and hate for Victor. Without warning, Anita kissed me as if I were her boyfriend. I knew it was part of her anger and the closeness we shared, and no doubt she needed a release for that moment. I was still very much in love with Anita, but I didn't want to take advantage of her. I didn't want her to do anything out of loneliness or desperation just to fulfill a temporary need, and I didn't know what to expect from her.

It was getting late. I started to leave, but Anita asked me to stay with her until her roommate returned. She said, "You're my friend, Charles, and I need to talk more about this and spend time with you before my mother and sister come. I want to come to grips with this thing."

Since Anita needed this time with me to get herself straight, I called in sick to my job and took the week off. Anita's mother and sister arrived and we helped them settle in their new apartment. It was so good to be with all of them again!

Anita and I stayed together that week. It was the first time we ever spent a lot of time together — really together. It was wonderful! Her roommate finally returned, and I had to get back to work and let Anita have the space she needed.

Over a year we saw each other a number of times and spent some days and weekends together — a real close friendship. She was working and getting on with her life. But I knew in my heart that she was still in love with Victor, or someone else. I couldn't figure it out.

Finally, she came to me and said, "Charles, I know what I'm about to say may hurt you, and I will always love you like a brother, but I've been seeing a Mexican man and living with him on weekends. He's 20 years older than I am and divorced. If I give you his papers, will you check him out for me?"

I was deeply surprised by this news, but I knew Anita was happy. I checked his papers for her and found them to be valid. We met once more and spent a weekend together. She was the only woman I had ever loved, and it would take me a long time to get over her. I knew wherever our lives would lead us, we were together in spirit. It was the last time Anita and I ever saw each other.

I took it very hard and did not date for almost a year. I got myself a dog whom I called Snoopy to keep me company. He took some of the loneliness away, especially when I came home at night.

VI

I wanted to get out of the city again and made arrangements for another job at Grossinger's. Work was plentiful with conventions and the regular weekend crowds. I even had the rare opportunity of meeting and serving Senator Robert F. Kennedy a month before he was killed by Sirhan Sirhan on June 5, 1968. (Sirhan was in my unit at Soledad Prison.)

Working at Grossinger's for a year, I saved lots of money but was still lonely and decided to move back to the city once more. I had enough money not to go to work for some time. I found a beautiful apartment on Schermerhorn Street near Brooklyn Heights and joined the Shelton Health Club, hoping to meet a nice lady.

At the club I noticed a really cute girl riding an exercise bicycle. She looked up and caught my eye — the attraction was immediate. Later we met in the snack bar, and she introduced herself as Donna Grafton from Burlington, Massachusetts. Having worked at Filene's in Boston, she was an assistant buyer at the Abraham and Strauss department store on Fulton Street. Donna, for some reason, knew I was shy and decided to make her own move. She wasn't fast at all, just honest, open, and friendly. We dated for a year, on and off, and gave each other a lot of space and respect. I had finally met someone I cared for, but I was keeping an open mind about it.

I saw Donna on the subway as I was coming home late one night (or rather, early in the morning — around 2:00). When I approached her, she seemed upset and depressed, though she denied any problem. I walked her home to be sure she was all right, kissed her, and went home.

A few days later I saw a friend of hers and expressed my concern for Donna. "Don't you know what happened?" her friend asked. "Donna's been going out with this guy in the Bronx. He got her pregnant and turned his back. The night you saw Donna on the train was the same day she got an abortion."

I took a long walk to think things out, and later as I was returning to my apartment, I could see someone sitting on the stoop. As I came nearer, I saw it was Donna with a suitcase, waiting for me. She immediately came into my arms and asked if she could stay with me for a few days. I knew she needed a friend and, of course, agreed. I decided not to tell her what I knew so that she could tell me on her own if she wanted to. For a moment I thought back to Anita — how I helped her, how she wanted my friendship. I wondered why a similar situation had come my way. It was fate, I guess.

Donna cried for hours but didn't talk much. She needed a friend and came directly to me. She told me only that she wanted to get her head straightened out, no more.

Weeks passed, and Donna seemed to feel better. We spent a lot of time together, but she never told me about the abortion. She decided to go back to Massachusetts. She wanted to further her career, she said, but I knew deep in my heart that she was running away from a bad experience.

I flew to Boston twice for visits and had hopes of rekindling our friendship. Donna admitted she really liked me, but she found a nice man who worked as truck driver and planned to marry him. She finally told me about the abortion, and as we parted for the last time, she said, "I wish it had been you, Charles." I returned to Brooklyn, again very lonely.

I started to wonder if anything was wrong with me and why everyone loved me like a brother only. I wanted to find happiness and true joy. I was always important to other people, but no one seemed to care enough about me to enter into the lasting relationship I wanted so badly.

VII

Another year and a half passed. I worked as a waiter in various restaurants in the city, but I hardly went out or dated.

In August 1971 I was sitting in an outdoor cafe when two girls walked past. One gave me a nice smile, and I decided not to pass up this opportunity. I waited until they came out of an ice cream parlour, then introduced myself to Marie Siderowicz and asked her for a date. To my surprise, especially since she didn't know me, she said yes.

We went to a restaurant where there was dancing and had a lot of fun. For sure, we were physically attracted to each other. Although Marie had a coarse personality, she seemed to like me a lot. I liked her too, and we both showed it. She had recently moved from Scranton, Pennsylvania, and wanted to find a life for herself. She loved the fast-moving pace of New York. I noticed how she would snap at people and criticize them, and I advised her to lay off this type of behavior. Since we really liked each other and both needed a relationship, I ignored the harsh side of Marie and wanted to get to know her better.

Marie was living with several other people, and they were about to be evicted for nonpayment of rent. I didn't want Marie to be out in the street and offered to help her. She was living week-to-week with her paychecks and had no savings. I had moved to Clinton Street in Cobble Hill, and I persuaded the landlord to give Marie an apartment near mine at an affordable rent.

I withdrew all the money I had in the bank ($700) and took Marie to the real estate office. She had her apartment the same day. I gave Marie some more money and told her to call me if she needed any other help. She got a roommate, and slowly they furnished their place. Marie was responsible, and I knew she wouldn't make me look like an idiot, vouching for her. I was happy I could help her. It always made me feel good to help other people.

I applied for a typesetting position at Young and Rubicam International on Madison Avenue, a complete change of pace for me. My yearly salary was peanuts compared to what I could earn in a restaurant, but it was a chance to learn the business, obtain health benefits, and have security.

Karl Goetz, the vice president of print operations, hired me. He was a nice man with little schooling, who came to America after spending five years in a German concentration camp. Karl and I were punctual and demanding of excellence, meeting our deadlines. In a year, Karl promoted me to be in full charge of my department. I developed my own techniques on the IBM Selectric composer and banged my head against the wall for months, for the pressures were great. Sometimes I worked through the night, though I never told Karl. I loved to see the final product that I created with the art directors. We were a team.

Though Marie and I dated, I started to see Terry, a girl from the ad agency. She approached me herself — a fast, smooth, manipulative woman — but I didn't catch it at first because of my instant physical attraction to her. We went out for four months, and she even had a key to my apartment.

One night in bed she said to me, "You're the best I have ever had sexually."

When I asked if that was all she was interested in, she replied, "Yes."

I told her to get dressed, led her to her car, and said, "We won't be going out any longer. In the end, you will only hurt me emotionally."

For a while, Terry tried to reconcile. I told her that she couldn't just use people for her own benefit and to find someone else who only wanted a fling. Terry was angry, but maybe I did her some good. I never found out, but I hoped maybe my values would rub off on her a bit.

I started to go out with Marie again, but I was not really happy. I don't know why, but maybe it was because of a loneliness I was born with or maybe God meant it to be this way.

I worked for Young and Rubicam for almost two years, but I was, as usual, very lonely. I seemed always to change jobs when I felt this way. I wanted to try living in California where the pace would be slower and people would smile when I did. Maybe I could be accepted as a person, not just for my appearance or professional talent. I was tired of the status quo and the phonies I worked with who tried to get ahead by using others. Some would sell out their own families for a promotion, a sick situation. I was too sensitive, too emotional, too caring and giving, and wondered why people acted this way.

Karl gave me a wonderful reference when I quit my job, and I moved into a YMCA uptown to save money until I could make arrangements to go to California. I took a temporary job for four hours a day until I left. Every penny counted.

Marie seemed upset that I was leaving New York, as if she really cared about me. I asked her to consider coming to California, but she didn't have the money to move. I told her I would write when I was settled, and if she wanted to come, I would send her a one-way ticket and spending money.

VIII

In January 1974 I arrived in San Francisco with the $5,000 I had saved. I rented a furnished apartment, registered with an employment agency, and bought a used car to get around. Marie agreed to come live with me, and I sent her the airline ticket. I told her whatever I had was hers also, and not to worry.

We spent the first couple of weeks going out every day and night, taking long drives down the coast, and just enjoying each other's company. It was like being married. Something about California made us both better individuals — more open, unlike New Yorkers.

We both went to work part-time, making money and finding new friends. Marie hit a great job with American Potato Company in San Francisco, and I worked for the Bechtel Corporation in the word processing/typesetting department. We moved to a less expensive apartment in Oakland.

After a while, though Marie and I continued to live together, our relationship waned. We were just going through the motions. Marie often made me extremely nervous by being opinionated, critical, and condemning of others. She always wanted her way, and it was difficult to sit down and talk to her. When I wanted to talk, she would plug her ears and go about her business. It bothered me a lot, and I always walked away from this kind of behavior. Yet Marie was a good person — at least I thought so, and still do.

We decided to try living apart until we could resolve our differences. I helped Marie find an apartment nearby. As usual, I helped her if she needed anything ... anything. I didn't see much of Marie for a while, but when I ran into her one day, she seemed angry. I knew why — we were not living together. I blamed myself, since I had asked her to come to California. I felt bad, really bad. She even said she was thinking of moving back to New York. I was shocked; I couldn't believe it. I wanted Marie to stay, and I think Marie wanted to stay, too. I could feel it inside myself.

Talking to Marie was difficult; she would hit hard with words. I couldn't understand her personality. It hurt me just to see her this way, abrasive and cruel. Her sister used to say, "Charles, you are going to have a lot of trouble with my sister one day. She's a hard person with words, but if you can accept it and love her, stay with her."

Marie didn't go back East, and we started living together again. Boy, was I happy about this! We were both working at jobs we enjoyed with decent salaries. I was then a typesetter at Pacific Rota Printing Company in Berkeley.

But loneliness set in deeply. I couldn't understand it. I wanted to return to New York, and so did Marie. Her family was there, and she missed them. Neither of us had much money. I decided the only way I could help people was to get a lot of money by forging some checks.

The company liked me and trusted me with a key to the building. One evening I entered the office and forged signatures on company checks made out to me totalling $23,000. I deposited them in my account, and, since the company's account was in the same bank as mine, they cleared overnight. I didn't tell Marie what I had done, as she surely would have been upset. She knew about my criminal record and that I had written checks over the years.

I told Marie I was ready to go to New York, and we packed and left without notifying our employers. We stayed at a hotel in Brooklyn Heights until I found an apartment at 130 Montague Street. Since we were still having problems with our relationship, we agreed to live separately again. I helped Marie find an apartment, paid a month's rent, and put money in her pocket.

Marie and I still dated, and I gave her money from time to time. I was negotiating a deal to buy a laundromat. I knew she was having a difficult time financially, and I wanted to help her in any way I could. I even took care of her when she was very ill with the flu.

Several months passed, and I saw Marie with a man she said was visiting from Canada and had a place nearby. She was watching his apartment while he was away on a business trip. A few days later I called her there, and the man was in the house. She explained that she might go to Canada with him, but I convinced her to talk to me before making a decision. I waited for her outside the building, and when she appeared, I blurted out, "Will you marry me?" She immediately said yes, and I knew then that, if she had gone to Canada, it would have been only out of loneliness and her need to get married.

We saw a doctor, got our blood tests and marriage license, and on February 21, 1975, Marie Siderowicz and I were married before a Justice of the Peace.

IX

We didn't have a honeymoon because four days after our wedding I completed the purchase of the laundromat at 68 Hicks Street. Since my criminal record would have made licensing difficult, I listed Marie as the sole owner. After all, she was my wife, and if anything ever happened to me, she would not be without. I was very concerned about helping Marie and pleasing her. She loved the almighty dollar.

I named the laundromat "The Washing Well" and closed it for a week for refurbishing. When we reopened, the first week's profits were $900—a wonderful beginning. I knew the neighborhood needed this valuable service, the only laundromat in the area. My deep desire to help people came to reality.

Soon after I opened up for the day on March 21, 1975, three men entered the laundromat. One of them flashed an FBI badge at me and placed me under arrest for the forgery I had committed months before in California. I was allowed to call Marie, and, needless to say, she was shocked since she didn't know about what I had done. I was lodged at the Brooklyn House of Detention to await an extradition hearing. Marie visited me and assured me she loved me and would never leave me.

A few days later my case was heard, and I flew back to Oakland, California, to stand trial. There I pleaded guilty and began a one-year sentence at the county jail at Santa Rita. However, three weeks later I was able to transfer to a work furlough program in Oakland. I worked during the day and returned to the furlough center at night.

Marie enlisted a friend, Margaret Tanner, to run the laundromat, and she moved to Oakland to be with me. She visited me every weekend, and things were much better for both of us emotionally. With special permission, I was able to visit Marie at her place.

During my incarceration at the furlough center, Marie got pregnant. How happy we were! But our business was not going well, and Marie had to go back. The money was not coming in as expected. I continued to work and sent Marie every penny I earned.

I hired an attorney to try to obtain an early release, and we were successful in our petition. So on Christmas Eve 1975, I flew back to New York.

Marie advised me that the business was still not going well. We had no money saved, and she had been trying to make ends meet and pay the employees. With Marie looking run down, it was time for me to take over. I was concerned about her health and wanted our child to be born healthy and on time with no worries. I never told Marie, but I used to go to a nearby church to ask God to take care of her and to pray for a healthy baby. I was always a private individual.

Margaret Tanner was a hard worker, but a manipulator. When I discovered she was doing work off the books and taking money under the table, I fired her. Marie was mad as hell because Margaret was her friend. She wouldn't talk to me for weeks until an extra $300 a week started coming in. Then she knew I had done the right thing and apologized.

The business was starting to pick up and was grossing $1,500 a week. But we had a lot of bills and still owed a lot of money. The lease on our laundromat was about to terminate, and I was getting worried about Marie, our child, and all the debts. The new lease would be expensive.

I thought about selling the business and looked into a loan. I needed a new lease in order to sell. I also had to pay back taxes, notes to the bank, Marie's medical bills, rent, food — you name it.

I continued to work hard and started to help the elderly by setting up a special senior citizens' day when they could wash and dry free once a week. The other three weeks were half-price. I also allowed any woman with a baby to wash the baby's clothes free for six months. The news spread quickly throughout Brooklyn, and the business was booming. I worked long hours. We still owed plenty of money.

After a few false alarms, on June 18, 1976, Marie started having serious contractions. I turned the shop over to the high school girls who worked for me and took Marie to the hospital. We had taken Lamaze classes so we could see our baby born together. Hours went by, and finally we went into the delivery room. I scrubbed and was dressed in gown, mask, and gloves. I immediately went over to Marie and kissed her through my mask. Who cared? I forgot everything. I was nervous.

I coached Marie with her breathing and pushing. At last, I saw a little baby boy pop out, and in just a few seconds, Marie and I heard our son, David, cry. The doctor placed him on Marie and told me to touch him. David was like paper. What a joy! God, I was so happy!

Marie was finally out of pain, and I was relieved. She had such a difficult pregnancy. I stayed with her until about 9:00 that night, then went to the laundromat where everyone was waiting for me. They had made a huge banner out of paper bags, and they were yelling, "Congratulations, Charles." A lot of people were there with lots of presents for David. I was so happy that I gave the help all the profits from that day. But I told them not to tell Marie, as she would never approve.

The next morning I went early to the hospital with a rose for Marie. (I gave her one yellow rose every week.) Marie was waiting for me with our son in her arms. All of a sudden she said, "I married you because I wanted a child. Now you support him." I was a little upset, but seeing how happy we were with David, I ignored her statement. You bet I was going to love and support our son!

We took David home to our apartment. We had very little furniture, and it didn't really look like the home we wanted; but I made sure David's room was furnished. I was really worried about how I would support Marie and our son. We owed so much money and had no savings.

Marie hemorrhaged from being on her feet too long. The doctor advised bed rest, so I hired a nurse for several weeks until she recovered. It cost plenty, but money was not the issue — it was Marie.

##

I finally sold the laundromat for $37,000, so we had plenty of money to take care of our son and furnish our apartment. I went to work almost right away as a waiter at Michael's Pub in Manhattan and was bringing in excellent money. But business slowed down, and I got laid off.

It was difficult to find work at this time, so I decided to buy another laundromat, which I called "Our Son's Place," about a block from our home. But before I closed the deal, I wanted David to be baptized as a Roman Catholic. So did Marie.

On September 19, 1976, David was baptized at St. Agnes' Church in Brooklyn. A few days later, my friend Father Duffy (who by then had been made a bishop) came over to the house and blessed our son. It meant so much to me. He didn't stay long, but I took him out for dinner a few weeks later. We always went out to dinner at least once a year to talk. It was a "must" for us. He was my father, the one I never had.

Buying this second laundromat was a big mistake. Marie told me not to buy it, and I should have listened to her. The building owners, whose names were Frank and Al, were extorting money from us for garbage disposal by requiring monthly checks made out to "cash." I knew something was wrong and talked to the disposal company. When they saw my cancelled checks, I received three months' free service, and the owners' monthly charge was doubled. I even went to the FBI about these men, but they weren't interested, perhaps because only $27 a month was involved. If it had been thousands, maybe they would have investigated. I did the best I could at the highest levels.

But I was mad. I took pictures of all the electrical and plumbing violations Al and Frank had in the basement, and I brought in an expert to examine the water pipes. Their business was connected to ours, and we were paying their water bills as well as some of their electric charges. Next I called the electric company, who discovered that Al and Frank had rigged their box to pay only $60 a month for a business whose electric bills should have amounted to $400 a month. They had to pay their back payments and a huge fine.

One day I was awakened by a phone call from Frank who told me the laundromat was on fire. By the time I got to the laundromat, the fire was out. The backs of the dryers were gone, and they needed new motors and support chains. The water damage was tremendous. The firemen said it was an electrical fire that started on Al's and Frank's premises.

Now I was mad as hell! Their insurance company examined the damage and sent us a check for only $943.50. Even though the fire started on their property, Al and Frank refused to do more. I went to their attorney who called for a meeting to resolve the problem. They tried to bribe me, and I walked out of the office. They brought me back and agreed to pay for the damages, to clear our credit, and to buy back the business — plus a $3,000 cash settlement. We lost a lot of money. I should have listened to Marie. I should have listened to my instincts.

I was deeply concerned about Marie's personality and attitude, and I needed to appease her. I was under a lot of pressure to supply her material needs. The value of the dollar didn't seem to mean anything to her. Her attitude was that everything was my responsibility.

XI

We discovered that Marie's mother had cancer. She was an alcoholic, never went to doctors, and had no medical insurance. Each time Marie needed to visit her in Scranton, she and David had to take a bus, then rent a car. It was very expensive. As a surprise for Marie, I bought her a brand new car so that she could get to her mother more easily. I paid cash and put it in her name.

I went to work as an assistant manager at The Gingerman, a restuarant in Manhattan. It didn't pay well, but I wanted to learn the restaurant business better. The responsibilities and hours were unbelievable — seven days a week. I hardly had time to see Marie or our son, but at least I was supporting them.

I couldn't wait to get home and pick up David. I did all sorts of things for him — rocked him, held him, changed his diapers, took him for walks, bought him toys. Seeing our son with his mother just made me overjoyed. David was everything to me. My job, regardless of Marie's coarse, sandpaper attitude, was to be responsible and committed. I was so proud to be a father. How I loved it!

Sometimes Marie would come after me with her mouth, never knowing when to zip it up. She said things like, "Fathers just don't do things like you do. You're abnormal." She thought it was outrageous that I would sing to David and dance him to sleep. Marie had a bad habit of yelling at me in front of our son, and it made him nervous.

One time when I came home from work, David had been crying for hours. I picked him up and sang to him, but Marie tried to grab David and told me I was spoiling him. I noticed David had been pulling on his ear, and I thought he might have an earache. Marie said, "He's not sick." I rocked David to sleep and took him to the doctor the next morning. Sure enough, he had an ear infection.

Over the months Marie's mother got worse, and the doctor wanted to do exploratory surgery. Without Marie's knowledge, I went to Scranton to talk with him. He said the operation was essential. I handed him an envelope with $3,000 cash in it, and asked him to do whatever was in his power to keep Marie's mother alive. He shook my hand and said, "I'll do my best." He promised not to tell Marie or her family of my efforts.

I was running out of money now. Marie didn't know how to control money. I often wondered how I could cope with her mouth, her abrasive and cruel remarks and behavior.

Marie flew to Scranton for her mother's operation. The doctor removed a softball-sized tumor from her colon, but the cancer had spread to other parts of her body. She withstood the operation well, though the prognosis wasn't good. I flew there to be with Marie and her brother and sisters. Within a few weeks, their mother went home. I was very upset about the conditions she was living in and wanted to help her.

On an impulse I went into the Gingerman office after closing hours, took some checks from the back of the book where it wouldn't be noticed, and forged checks worth $29,000. I opened an account with them at a nearby bank, and in three days the checks cleared. I waited for a few more days, and on June 23, 1978, I tried to withdraw all the money.

Within minutes I was surrounded by plainclothes police officers and placed under arrest. They took me to the police station, booked me, and I was back in the Brooklyn House of Detention. When I called Marie to tell her what happened, she was very angry and told me she was going to get a divorce.

On September 17, 1978, Marie's mother died. I was upset about her death. I tried like hell to help her, but my efforts had failed.

Marie came to see me in jail only once, and she asked me again for a divorce. I told her if she filed, I would consent; but I was totally against divorce in every way.

Before my sentencing, I told Marie where to find the key to my safe deposit box and signed authorization for her to open it. I left her with $20,000 cash, plus the car. At least that would help her and our son. Marie called me a lot of names because I got myself in trouble and hung up on me many times. After all, I did get in trouble with the law and left her with the burden of taking care of our son alone.

I was sentenced to two to four years at a New York State prison for forgery, and on December 4, 1978, I received a judgment of divorce. I didn't know if I would see my son again. ∎

Analysis I
Jack Wilson

Charles Rothenberg's description of his early years shows that the context for the development of his own conscience, healthy self-esteem, sense of belonging, and religious concepts was sorely lacking. Consistent, stable, loving parent-figures usually provide the keys for growth in these areas. Charles did not have them.

Consider the issue of conscience. Conscience develops as children learn what is acceptable and unacceptable from their parents. These standards need consistency through the developmental years. Depth of conscience evolves as the bond children feel for their parents causes them to want to please as well as to fear their disapproval. And a healthy conscience helps a child to come to terms with the Christian religion in ways that go beyond shallow association.

Many Bible stories taught in church schools have strong moral overtones. Stories of God's blessing those who remain loyal regardless of outside pressures such as Daniel in the lion's den, or those who demonstrate honesty and integrity such as Joseph in captivity in Egypt are colorful illustrations of the Old Testament's moral viewpoint. The New Testament, too, contains moral guidance. Most are aware that the "golden rule" derives from the New Testament. And the standards held forth by Jesus in the "Sermon on the Mount" address not just external behavior, but attitudes of the heart as well.

To develop a healthy self-concept, a child needs continued reassurance and affection from his/her parents. The sense of worth that grows in such a loving context is based not on performance or appearance but simply on the fact of a child's existence. A sense of belonging, the opposite of loneliness, comes primarily from the bond the child feels with his/her family through the early years. When self-esteem and a sense of belonging are absent, the Christian message of repentance[1] is often heard as a message of rejection rather than as part of the message of redemption, and it drives one to hide from God or the church. If the notion of repentance is ignored and opportunities for involvement and group experience are offered unconditionally, low self-esteem and the need to belong will drive one to seek only those aspects of God or the church that provide "warm fuzzies."

Charles' account of his relationship with his childhood friend Timmy lays bare the result of his undeveloped and unmet needs of

---

[1] Acts 3.19.

belonging, and foreshadows his adult behavior as well. Charles helped Timmy with his schoolwork by cheating for him. The reason? So that Timmy wouldn't get bad grades, be demoted from the class, and thus be separated from Charles. This ability to do wrong in order to feel connected with others became a hallmark of Charles' life. Later he was able to lie, cheat, and steal in order to "help" others with whom he had relationships.

Parent metaphors for God, particularly "father," are prominent in religious teachings and writings. Charles had no consistent father-figure who loved him as well as disciplined him through his formative years. Thus the term "father," when heard in a religious context, would have elicited a mixed reaction: his father had abandoned him, yet Charles continued to yearn for him. Charles claims he was taught how to obey, take orders, and respect others, but he was taught by "house parents," and doesn't even mention their names.

Charles' description of his mother shows almost total disconnectedness: she was unaffectionate, uncommunicative, and uninterested in offering him the special experiences that parents normally give their children. He openly admits that he had great difficulty answering the question "Do you have a family?" in his early years, blocking his circumstances from his mind.

A child whose parents are supportive and caring in times of extreme distress gains further thought-forms to employ in thinking independently about God; but Charles lacked such experiences. When Charles was hospitalized, his mother came to see him only once; his house parents were far more attentive, visiting twice a week. Whatever Charles learned of God's "grace to help in times of need"[2] did not come from his parents.

In spite of his obviously disrupted early life, Charles characterizes his time in two orphanages as "a normal upbringing," a remark that might be expected from someone who desperately needs to feel "normal."

Charles encountered religious institutions and ministers through his early years, mostly as sources for help when in need and as providers of group experiences. Earliest descriptions of his experiences that may be called religious are of participation in activities at the Woodycrest Home associated with Christmas. While he notes that he attended church and Sunday School at the Chapel of the Intercession, it was his participation in the Christmas pageant, singing in the choir and playing on the church basketball team that stand out in his mind. Rev. Jennings, the rector, helped Charles a great deal. These experiences potentially communicated something of the mercy and love of God to Charles. On the other hand, they may have reinforced to Charles the notion that the church is there only to provide happy circumstances and needed help.

---

[2] Hebrews 4.16

What appears to be missing from Charles' experience with religion is any sense of doctrine. He would later be able to flip back and forth between different Christian traditions, with apparently no concept of doctrinal or practical differences. And any notion of the awe of God appears to be completely lacking.[3]

Despite frequent allusions to relationships with religious persons or institutions, conspicuously lacking are references to any cognitive development in matters of religion. Charles summarizes his spiritual instruction with a statement that on the surface may appear complete: *"I was taught to give for Him and to others; to love Him and others; to be obedient to Him and to others; to pray to Him and for others; to be kind, share, and forgive."* The practical meaning he gave to each phrase, however, was far from uniform. Any sense of morality paled in the light of ideas of giving and sharing.

Prayer appears to be, at least in these early years, a rote exercise employed to make Charles feel better. Further, helping others seems to be the mechanism that helped Charles feel like he belonged, like he was somebody. He describes himself at this time as being very lonely and impulsively helping people. The impulses that drove him to cheat or steal to help another obviously did not come from a desire to do the right thing or to please God. And when I asked Charles if he had any thoughts of God or God's judgment while he contemplated and perpetrated his crime, he answered "No."

During his stay in Puerto Rico, Charles developed a relationship with Father Michael Duffy with whom he apparently had many conversations. He portrays Father Duffy as a warm, loving and gracious man of God, but his association with this religious leader seems not to have included moral suasion or accountability. At least that was Charles' impression.

Later, when Charles was in Sing Sing, he recalls that Father Duffy encouraged him never to give up hope and to believe that God forgives. At that point Charles was using the rosary and attending Roman Catholic services in the prison. Any doctrinal differences between his early training in the Episcopal church and the teachings of the Roman church weren't an issue. His need to belong and the unconditional acceptance and availability of the Roman Catholic services made those differences irrelevant. It is not that one primarily raised in an Episcopal tradition cannot worship in a Roman Catholic service. Though people may worship occasionally in other traditions, they usually stay within their own, unless a conscious conversion to another takes place. Charles never indicates such a change, and he was able to casually flip back and forth, no doubt driven by his need to belong.

---

[3] The book of Proverbs is often used as part of the biblical material used in instructing children. One of its basic messages is, "The fear of the Lord is the beginning of wisdom." Proverbs 1:7.

From his own description, Charles looks like a young man who used religion to meet certain emotional needs. There's nothing immoral or even unusual about that, but religion is more than water for emotional thirst. Most religious traditions help people be good, not just feel good, combining a strong moral message with the deeds of love and mercy that a church extends. If such a message was given to Charles, he apparently was unable to process it. ■

Andrew Savicky

Charles Rothenberg's childhood was an interaction of fantasy and real life. He seemed to exist in a dreamlike state of projected happiness, but always with underlying themes of depression, sacrifice, and pain.

He paints a rosy picture of his life at the Woodycrest Home and calls himself *"extremely fortunate"* to be there. He writes of having a *"fine upbringing,"* of being treated with *"love and respect,"* of house parents and other personnel who were *"deeply caring,"* of experiences such as camp, school, and outings that were *"exciting"* and *"fun"* — and says he was *"so very grateful."*

The reality is that Charles probably had a childhood devoid of positive emotional contact. Abandoned in an orphanage, he no doubt had many unmet developmental needs, disappointments, and a poor self-image. Yet for his own self-protection, he describes the home as a nice place to grow up and makes himself out as well-adjusted.

Charles says he was treated like a *"normal kid."* He makes it a point to deny any physical abuse, though he reports a *"ruler over our butts or the palms of our hands"* for disobedience, indicating that he may indeed have been abused.

He seemed to enjoy the limelight on the basketball team and in the Christmas pageant, which suggests his need for recognition. (Later Charles would leave clues so that his crimes were easily traced to him — negative recognition was better than none.) His description of himself is filled with positive and desirable character traits, and this need to communicate how wonderful he is probably points to his low self-esteem and compensates for what he didn't have. He wanted so much for people to like him and approve of him.

Charles' cheerful narrative of his early years is marred by references to his family, particularly his mother. Even here he continues to attempt to depict his life as upbeat and positive, but she regularly disappointed and rejected him. It is clear that the relationship he desperately wanted with his mother just didn't exist and was instead an extremely painful one.

His relationship with his mother is key to so many of the problems that afflicted Charles throughout his life, and his masochistic tendencies can likely be traced to this source. In all his other relationships Charles, in one way or another, repeated the theme of his relationship with his mother. If a relationship was positive at the outset, Charles would find a way to sabotage it and make it negative, emulating the failed primary relationship in his life and confirming that pain was what he deserved. And pain is what he sought over and over again.

Charles' mother seldom visited him at the orphanage or even when he was in the hospital, and their limited time together seemed always to be unsatisfactory. Though he claims she never gave him affection, displayed her love, or even chatted like a friend, Charles professes his love for her again and again and does not verbalize his anger or hurt. Her life as a prostitute set an example for Charles and taught him to do anything for a fee: he could be anything he wanted to be, at a cost. Certainly she provided no role model for honesty.

The shattering of Charles' idealization of his mother is repeated by her frequently abandoning him. His inability to endure that loss had a profound impact on both his emotions and intellectual thinking. After he left the orphanage, Charles lived with his mother only briefly before he discovered her "life-style" and went to Massachusetts in the care of his uncle. Even after she insisted that he return, she could not care for him and consigned him to life in a state institution where his peers were juvenile delinquents. Later when Charles was earning a living, he gave his mother money, told her he loved her, and attempted to persuade her to live with him, still trying to create what he wished he had had in his life.

Upon learning of his mother's death, Charles was probably ambivalent, but guilt was paramount. He may have wished her death on some level or may have felt he could have prevented it if he had been a better person. But her death only intensified his need for a mother figure.

Charles never knew his father, and this abandonment probably caused him to search for situations in which he would find that missing father figure. When Charles felt abandoned throughout his life, he (the dependent child) often tried to create relationships where he could have the missing figure (a caring and supportive parent) available to him. His relationships with Rev. Jennings, Tom, Father Duffy, and even Harry Gaynor are examples.

Charles describes his uncles as well-educated and having prominent professions, establishing a connection with an education he never attained. He claims his uncles proposed to send him to military school and then on to Harvard University to become a doctor, though his mother refused. Here Charles makes a strong attempt to validate his self-worth by suggesting how his life would have been different if the circumstances had been right, but he probably believed that he was simply not worthy of what had been promised.

We learn little of Charles' childhood friends, but his friendship with Timmy was typical of other relationships still to come. Charles describes Timmy's personality as like that of Don Rickles, a comedian whose trademark is insults, sarcasm, and put-downs. His cheating for Timmy is an early indication of his pattern of helping people by dishonest means in his search for approval and acceptance through self-sacrifice.

In his late teens Charles secured his first permanent employment, and here we can discern the masochistic pattern that he would follow in many areas of his life. He reports that he liked his job at Grossinger's, that he worked hard, earned good wages, and was reliable and well-liked. In addition, this job gave structure to his time, which was familiar from his institutional upbringing and probably helped him to feel secure. Nonetheless, Charles claims that he was lonely — by choice, it seems, and not circumstance, though Charles often blames circumstances for his predicaments rather than taking responsibility himself. Then as if his life were too good and thus he had to change it for the worse, he quit his job and returned to New York.

Charles was able to recognize his feelings of loneliness and depression, but since he felt they were deserved, he didn't deal with them. He could never allow things to go well in his life; indeed, he needed to fail. Whether a job or a relationship, as soon as it started to go well, he did something to transform success into failure, filtering all his experience through his childhood pain.

Charles' relationships with women also fit a predictable model. He developed a happy relationship with Anita, which also gave him a sense of the family he never had. He describes himself in heroic terms: chasing away Pilar's drunken husband, buying food for the family, giving them money, and going to work to support them. Yet Charles put an end to this presumably happy scenario by stealing to "help" the family. He justifies this crime by telling of the family's need and takes no responsibility; nonetheless, his behavior put him in a painful situation.

Later he allowed himself to be used by Anita as he supported her emotionally and helped her get established in New York. His fear of rejection led him to put her in a position of accepting him because of all he did for her; so with Charles as a willing participant, she took advantage of him and eventually left him anyway. His relationships with Donna and Terry ran along the same lines, both ending painfully for Charles.

In his early crimes of stealing travelers checks in Puerto Rico and attempting a robbery at Grand Central Station, Charles set himself up to be caught and consequently sent to jail. The consistency and safety of the structure of institutional care was comfortable for him; he liked having others tell him what to do. He disassociated himself from the other inmates, which was probably a defense mechanism to remove himself from responsibility for his circum-stances and for his wrongdoing. He probably could have avoided his extradition to Puerto Rico, but he chose instead to "do [his] time." It was important for him to survive the pain of jail, overcoming adversity and coming out a hero.

When Charles met Marie, the old patterns emerged once again. Though he thought Marie was coarse and critical (abusive like his mother? insulting and sarcastic like his boyhood friend Timmy?), he quickly set to work to be her hero by giving her money and helping her rent an apartment. He had a good job and was involved in this relationship, but he says he was lonely and depressed. The status quo was good, so he had to move on. When Charles proposed to move to California, he had an opportunity to end the relationship with Marie, but he reverted to passivity and relinquished control, leaving it up to Marie if she wanted to come to California with him.

They had their ups and downs, but both Charles and Marie had jobs and seemed to be happy in California. As usual, however, Charles couldn't handle happiness. He committed a forgery (an easily traceable crime for which he was later arrested and imprisoned) and they moved back to New York.

Perhaps Charles was afraid of losing Marie. Perhaps he needed to be in an abusive relationship that probably reminded him of his mother. *"Opinionated, abrasive," "cruel,"* and at the same time *"a good person"* are words with which he describes Marie. Whatever the reason, Charles and Marie were married. For once it seemed that Charles would sustain a relationship, but the wedding only post-poned its painful conclusion.

David's birth was apparently an occasion of great joy for Charles, yet when he first touched David, he says David felt like paper. Did he think of David as a "thing" that could be owned, destroyed, disposed of, thrown away? He later states that *children are the greatest commodity we have in life,"* as if children were simply objects.

Charles portrays himself as a model husband and father, working long hours to support his family and being extremely attentive to David. He also tried to be a hero during his mother-in-law's illness and ultimately committed another forgery, ostensibly to help her. As usual, his guilt was easily discovered. This time, however, his punishment was not only a jail sentence but also a divorce, leaving David without his father. ■

Charles Rothenberg
Struggles

I

Once again, I was in Sing Sing. I went through the classification process and was stuffed into a cell. The inmates were mostly black and Hispanic, and most of the officers seemed to be the same.

Three weeks later I was transferred to the Clinton Correctional Facility in Dannemora, New York, about 500 miles from New York City. It appeared that the pre-programming I was about to receive would be rough — a 90-day stress program — and I was scared.

About 80 of us were put into separate cells in a unit completely closed off from the general prison population. Then we went to the barber shop and had our heads shaved. One imate refused, and he was brutally beaten by two officers in front of the rest of us. (Another inmate who had refused to carry a bag off the bus was beaten and never seen again. Rumor had it that he died of a heart attack.) We showered, dressed in the new clothes we received, and lined up against the wall for a briefing by the captain.

The captain told us that we would remain in this unit for about 90 days while we had all kinds of tests and then would be reassigned. He advised us that if we disobeyed an order, there would be no second chances. If we didn't know what he meant, the officers who started banging their sticks against the wall made his words very clear. I eventually entered a special program for inmates with minor offenses and had advantages that the general population did not have. It was really comfortable! I couldn't believe it! However, if an inmate abused his privileges, his participation in the program ended as quickly as it began.

A few months went by, and I heard nothing from Marie, though I had written to her. I started to get nervous, not hearing how David was doing. I told the officer on duty about my problem, and I was sent to the hospital for a check-up. I was not sick physically and knew the institution was playing with my mind. When I went back to my cell, a letter from Marie was on my bed. Nervously I opened it and read that David was okay and that she was dating a New York City police officer, John Cirillo. The letter was not long, but I felt better.

Many months passed, and I seldom heard from Marie, though I wrote frequently. When she did write, the letters were cold and sometimes not signed, but she gave me news about our son. She always brought up her boyfriend and the places they went. Sometimes I received photos of David, which made my day. I was reluctant to tell Marie that I wanted to know more about David because of her hard personality. When I did ask, her next letter would say only that her boyfriend was taking care of them. At least I knew that everything was okay.

I didn't just serve time at Clinton; I used it to my advantage. I talked a lot to my counselor about the years I had written bad checks. I realized that I loved the dollar bill, and it always got me in trouble. I just wasted the years and lost many friends. I always wanted to help people and knew this was the reason I wanted so much money.

My faith and belief in God surely got stronger as well as my desire to go back into the community to work and support my son and help Marie. I worried a lot about Marie's personality, how coarse she was and the way she used to dig her mouth and teeth at me. Sometimes she made me feel less than human. I wondered what it would be like with another man in her life and how it would affect my relationship and fatherly rights with David.

Nearly two years after my crime, I prepared to meet with the Parole Board. Before I could obtain a release date, I had to find a suitable program to present to them. I had no money and no one to help me, but during my incarceration I became very close to the Catholic priest and to God. I knew everything would be okay.

An inmate suggested that I write to an attorney he knew. It was Roy M. Cohn, the lawyer who had represented Senator Joseph McCarthy in 1954. Mr. Cohn agreed to help me with a recommendation for my release and a reference for work.

I also had to find a place to live. Marie refused to let me stay with her for a few days and told me I would have make it on my own. I contacted Bishop Duffy, and he arranged for me to stay at a Catholic residence in Manhattan for $55 a week.

The problem still was to raise money so that the Parole Board would see that I could be released and take care of myself without stealing or writing checks. Three weeks before my hearing, I received a money order for $800 from someone whose name I did not recognize in Ohio, with no letter or return address. This was crazy. Who the hell would just send me money without knowing me?

I was worried about the hearing. I had seen inmates take an approved plan to the Parole Board and get shot down without any reason. My counselor seemed to have high hopes because I was in for a white-collar crime. If I didn't make it, I knew another seven months would take their toll on me. I wanted to get out and support my boy!

Waiting outside the hearing room seemed interminable. When I went inside, I faced a panel of three men who just looked at their files. Then one said, "Mr. Rothenberg, we've decided to give you a chance and release you on June 23rd. Hopefully, you will not return, for if you do, you will serve the maximum sentence allowed by law. We see that you have enough money and, with your previous experience, will be able to find a job."

I thanked them and left the room happy that my time at Clinton would soon be over.

I got special permission to call Marie. It was the first time in two years that we had heard each other's voices. She acted business-like and was not very nice. I heard David in the background, but she wouldn't let me speak to him. Marie told me that John didn't like me and didn't want me around. She said that she thought John was right and would do anything for him.

II

On June 23, 1980, I left Clinton on a bus for Manhattan. Marie refused to meet me at the bus station, but I made an appointment to see David a few days later. All my clothes were at her place, and I wanted to secure a temporary job as soon as possible so I could start supporting David and Marie. I bought David a farm game for $60 — a bit expensive, but I wanted to get him something nice since I hadn't seen him for two years.

I rang Marie's bell at 382 Court Street in Brooklyn at the appointed time. There was my son at the top of the stairs, smiling and shouting, "Mommy, here comes Daddy."

Marie came to the door looking stern and upset. I guess we were all a little nervous and didn't know what to say. I went into the living room and gave David his present. He was really happy and came into my arms, kissing me right and left and just looking at me with his big eyes. He ran back to his new toy and tried to put it together. He was only four years old, and I helped him.

Marie started to act more decent and offered me a cup of coffee. For two hours David and I just played. He showed me his room and his toys and kept asking me, "When are you coming again, Daddy?" I answered, "Whenever Daddy and Mommy work it out."

I handed Marie $40 (although she said to keep it until I got settled if I needed it) and agreed to give her $50 each week for support. I knew $50 was not enough, and I planned to give her more once I got a good job.

Before I left, I picked up my son, kissed him, and told him how much I loved him. David just looked at me, and I could tell in his eyes that he was happy. It was a happy day for me, too, and all I could think about was to get to work and help my son and visit him. It would be tough for a while, but I was determined to make it!

Through a temporary agency, I immediately secured a secre-tarial job with the Ford Foundation at $6 an hour. I worked there for two weeks, but once taxes were withheld from my paycheck, I could scarcely cover my expenses. So I quit and applied for a waiter's position at Leo's Coffee Shop on East 86th Street.

I called Marie to ask to visit with my son, but she and her boyfriend had already made plans to go to Vermont for the weekend. I inquired if my son had asked for me. She said he had, but that was too bad. Marie was surprised to hear that I had $50 for her. She thought it would be a while before I could pay support, but I wanted to begin right away. She started to get nice and asked me to come to Brooklyn, not to see our son but to leave the money in her mailbox. Well, I did, but I also rang the bell. They were still there, and I went up to see David, who jumped into my arms and asked, "Is Daddy coming with us?" Marie introduced me to John Cirillo, a strong man with a firm handshake. Marie thanked me for the money and told me to call the following week.

I worked at Leo's day and night to make ends meet. I worked six days a week and started to save money. The manager was nasty, and sometimes it was uncomfortable even to come to work, not knowing what he might say or do. I wanted to quit, but I stayed on until I had another job to assure a steady income.

I called Roy Cohn to ask him to help me find a job. His secretary, Sandra Wolfe, suggested that I go to the Silver Star Restaurant on East 65th Street, as the owner was always looking for good, reliable waiters and the money would be excellent. I made an appointment that same evening, was hired, and started work the next day.

The first week went very well, and the money was great. I had a six-day schedule and worked a lot of hours, but I also wanted time to spend with David. To be nearer my son, I rented a room for $30 a week only a few blocks from Marie and David. I waited for a month to tell Marie about my job change and move. I also told her I would be giving her $10 more a week. She was upset that I moved nearby because of her boyfriend, but David was happy and that was all that mattered to me. Marie was concerned that I would come around too much. I told her that I moved only to be near my son and that I would not get in the way of her relationship with John. The $10 a week seemed to appease her, as money always did, so I was happy.

III

Months went by, and with long hours at the Silver Star I was saving a lot of money, supporting my boy and Marie, and helping out in any way I could. I continued to see David. Once he stayed overnight in my room, but the landlord got upset. He was an elderly man, and because of his age he often said things he probably didn't mean.

Christmas was coming, and I wanted it to be a good one, not only for my son but for Marie as well. I decided to give Marie $500 to buy our son's Christmas presents. I went to the building where she worked and called her from the pay phone in the lobby, asking her to come down to see me. Boy, was she mad! When she came out of the elevator, she shouted, "Why are you here, Charles?" I gave her the envelope with the money in it and asked her to request a day off so I could take her shopping. Marie gave me a kiss on the cheek, and for the moment I was a good guy to her.

A few days later we purchased David's gifts at a toy store. A little money was left, so we went to lunch and Marie kept the rest. We went back to her place and wrapped all the presents, then hid them from David.

I made arrangements to be there at 5:00 Christmas morning while David was still asleep so he could see his parents together. Sure enough, David got up about about 6:00 and ran directly to the tree. He was so cute! We had to help him open everything. I could stay only an hour, as John was coming over and Marie wanted me out of the house. That hour went by so quickly, but it made my day! As I left, I hugged both David and Marie and handed Marie a $50 bill. She didn't know what to say, I guess, but I knew she was always happy when the buck was there. Marie asked me many times over the years why I helped her so much. But I couldn't change and never wanted to in this area.

After the holidays I found an apartment at 194 Court Street, about 10 blocks away from my son. The building was old and the rent cheap, and at last David could have his own place to stay with me. I spent almost everything I had in the bank to fix it up and bought an answering machine in case David or Marie wanted to leave a message. David memorized the phone number.

I wanted to let David see Marie and me together more often, though Marie was against this idea because of John. Without telling her, I purchased three tickets for "Peter Pan" on Broadway. Marie was mad as hell, but when I offered to give her a day's pay plus dinner for all of us, she agreed to go. David had a wonderful time, and of course I participated in his joy. Marie, although I believe she liked the show, didn't reveal her feelings and just sat there.

Another time I tried to get her to come with us to the circus at Madison Square Garden, but she refused. She let David go because he kept telling Marie that he wanted to be with me. I bought David everything he wanted, and why not? My son had the right as a child to experience life with his Dad.

I asked Marie if I could walk my son to his day care center in the morning before going to work. At first she said no because she was paying a friend to take him, but I later found out that Marie had told the teachers I was in prison and was embarrassed for them to see me. David wanted me to walk him, and I finally convinced Marie to let me do it three times a week. Boy, was I happy! I would leave David at the school, and he would go to the window and wave to me. On my day off I would sometimes pick him up and treat him to dinner at Helen's, an Italian restaurant nearby, before taking him home. Since John was usually there, Marie just didn't want me around, and she would make a point of this in front of our son. As usual, I walked away from her verbal abuse.

David was starting to become somewhat unresponsive to me, and I wanted to discuss this problem with Marie. When I was arguing with her over the phone about money and heard David crying, "Why are you yelling at Daddy?" I knew I had to talk to her and made arrangements to meet her for lunch on January 19, 1981.

On a whim I purchased a tiny tape recorder, and as we sat in the restaurant, the recorder was in my shirt pocket with the tape running. It was a pleasant lunch, and Marie seemed to be enjoying the meal. All of a sudden, she looked at me and said, "Charles, would you consider giving David up for adoption so that when I marry John, he can be his father?"

She continued, "You are only a waiter, and John is a police officer who has the respect and admiration of the public. I feel he would be a better father and would provide for David more. You've been in trouble with the law all your life, and if David knew of your past, he wouldn't want to see you. I love John and would do anything for him. David will forget you in time."

I was shocked and outraged, but I didn't show it. I knew I had to see David right away. I loved him so much! I walked Marie back to her job, then picked up David at school. He spent the night with me and went back to school in the morning.

A few days later Marie asked to see me. With David playing nearby, she said in a loud tone, "I want $75 a week, or you can't see David." I said I would try, but my financial situation wasn't good. Again she demanded the $75. We started to argue, and Marie threatened to call the police if I didn't get out. David was crying, and I told Marie to stop yelling at me in front of our son. I left quickly because I was so concerned about the effect these threats were having on David.

Things were getting tough for me. I couldn't control Marie's personality or her mouth. Every time she screamed at me, John's name came up. "He's a cop, and don't forget it," she would say. I had to do something, and so I began searching for legal assistance.

I went to Joe Di Napoli, an attorney Marie and I had known for years. I made a copy of the taped conversation in the restaurant for him, and when he heard it, he was mad as hell. Joe advised me to take Marie to court and get reasonable visitation rights and support payments. We did this, and the judge set $50 a week for support (though I often gave Marie $75) and made it clear that I was to have visitation with David. Things were still not right, however, as Marie and John were going away with David without telling me. David always wanted to see me, but he had no control. In a way, neither did I.

Next I wrote a long letter outlining my problems to Roy Cohn, and when I called his office, I talked with his secretary. She said that Mr. Cohn would write to Marie on my behalf.

I had also seen another attorney, Wayne Price, after Marie and John took David off to Florida when I already had permission from my parole officer and David's teacher and had made reservations to take David to Disney World. He, too, wrote to Marie about my visitation rights.

For months I continued to have difficulties with Marie and John. One night I called John at home, and he said right out, "I will do what Marie wants. Women always win out, you know." He told me that he and Marie didn't like me and didn't want me around.

IV

Well, things got still worse. I would stand outside Marie's apartment waiting to walk David to school, but he didn't appear and no one answered the bell. One night I waited outside the 13th Precinct to try to talk with John as he was going to work. Since he was Marie's boyfriend, I wanted to straighten things out and let him know my concern was only for my son and nothing else. John's buddies started to assemble around us, but John assured them everything was okay, and we walked down the street.

I told John that Marie was not letting me see David unless I gave her the money she demanded and that she wasn't showing up when we arranged appointments. He said that he wasn't going to get involved, but Marie was his girlfriend and he would support anything she decided. When I asked him about the adoption, he again stated that he would support Marie. I was mad as hell, and I started yelling at him.

John told me that he had problems with his ex-wife and that he often couldn't see his own two sons. But he said he wouldn't fight it because judges always go the woman's way and he couldn't win. I called him a chicken. If he loved his children the way I loved David, he would take his ex-wife to court. But John said, "I'm not going to fight like you. It's not worth it. Now I'm looking out for myself, and Marie is a part of that."

I made it clear to John that I was interested only in David and that I would never, I mean never, give him up for adoption. If the problems persisted, Marie would keep hearing from my attorneys, and they would just have to adjust to the fact that I was David's father and would be around.

This adoption issue really bothered me. It was on my mind quite a lot, and I couldn't sleep every time I thought about it. I listened to the tape recording over and over again and wondered why Marie would even think of such a thing. I used to walk for hours on end thinking about it and crying. I often called Roy Cohn's secretary, and if it hadn't been for her listening and caring, I really believe I would have gone off the handle.

I continued to work very hard and often saw David only for a few minutes in the morning when I walked him to the day care center. Many times he wanted to talk to me, but I usually didn't get the message from my answering machine until 14 to 16 hours later when I came home from work, and by then it was too late.

My solution to this problem was to buy a beeper so that as soon as David called me, I would know it and I could call him back. Marie thought I was out of my mind, but I gave her the dialing information anyway. She had not been aware of David's calls, and when she considered it, she realized that the beeper was not such a bad idea after all.

John and Marie were having a lot of personal problems and broke off their engagement on a number of occasions. John asked me why Marie was such a difficult and hardened individual. He claimed he never could sit down and talk to her without being rebuffed. I replied that if he loved her, he should accept her as she was.

One morning when I picked up David, Marie invited me upstairs for a cup of coffee and asked me to take David for six months a year. She started to yell at me in front of our son, saying that she had had enough and wanted time for her own life without taking care of a child. When I asked if she was having problems with John, she admitted that she had broken off the engagement. I knew that she had said these things out of anger, so I just told her that I thought our son needed his mother, though I would always be there. I reiterated that I was the one paying the bills, and if she needed money, she had only to ask.

On August 1, 1982, I got up early to go to the day care center just to see David briefly and to tell him I loved him before I went to work. Though Marie and John were still having problems, they were back together, at least for the time being. As I approached the school, I saw John and David walking down the street holding hands. When I said hello, John raised his fist and yelled, "Get away from here." David pulled away from John, scared. John grabbed me around the throat and warned me to leave Marie and him alone or he'd punch me right there in front of David. Two teachers who heard the commotion told John that he had no right to tell me to get away from the center and to leave himself. He took David into the school. I followed them, kissed my son, and left. I saw my son's face — he didn't know what to do.

I went inside again after John left. The director and his secretary were so understanding and sympathetic. I told them I would take the day off and come back to pick up David after school because I thought he needed me. They totally agreed.

I walked back to my apartment and called Marie. (I turned on the recorder, as I had started to tape all our conversations now. I'm not sure why, but I believe I was trying to understand Marie's mouth and her personality.) Before I could recount the scene at the school, she said, "I know, John already called me. I was hoping the day would come when John would kill you or hurt you. Now will you leave us alone? We don't want you around. Don't you understand, Charles? You're scum, and we both hate you. You're no good, nothing but a criminal." Then she hung up. I couldn't get a word in. It was no use.

I also called Joe Di Napoli, who was outraged when he heard my story and the tape of my conversation with Marie. He advised taking Marie and John to court, but I was against it for David's sake. I was concerned about Marie's temper, and I wasn't sure what John would do behind the scenes. After all, he had a badge and a gun. Joe wrote to John and put him on notice not to threaten me or interfere with my visitation rights. Joe encouraged me never to back off from them and to fight on.

Another call to Marie, and I had her permission to pick up David and keep him overnight. He seemed so pleased that we would be together the rest of the day. The teachers were glad, too; they knew my son needed me. I thanked them all for coming to my aid that morning. David and I spent a wonderful afternoon in Central Park, seeing the animals and eating hot dogs and popcorn.

That night Marie called and let me have it again. She said I was a bad father and didn't give her enough money. She and John wished I were dead. Whenever I tried to speak, she cut me off. Every time Marie talked to me this way I got nervous, but I wasn't about to walk away. David was my son! I spent the rest of the night crying and trying to figure out why Marie and John were after me and how to make them see that, as David's father, I had to be around.

V

It was almost time for David to enter first grade at P.S. 58, and Marie was having difficulty placing our son in an after-school program that would pick him up after school and care for him until she came home from work. She was angry because she thought I wasn't helping, but as it turned out, I was able to enroll David in a center just down the street. Marie was grateful, and I took that opportunity to request seeing her and David together.

I had been planning and working for this occasion for a long time. I told Marie in David's presence that I was going to pick up the payments for the after-school program as well as David's total support — food, clothing, medical expenses — everything, regardless of the cost.

Marie couldn't understand why I would make this offer, but I simply said, "David is my son. I love him, and I want to support him. If you are without, our son suffers, and I am not allowing that ever to happen."

I was working all kinds of hours, and I wanted David to know it was all for him.

On David's first day of school, I got up early and called in sick to my job. As I walked toward the school, I saw Marie, John, and David coming down the street. David ran to me, and we walked hand-in-hand to the schoolyard where all the new children gathered. I attended a discussion for parents, then sat in David's class for a few minutes. Marie and John had gone. I gave the school office my home and beeper number in case of emergency.

As the weather grew colder, David needed winter clothes. Marie took a day off (I gave her a day's pay), and we went to Macy's where we purchased everything David needed. I even bought Marie a pocketbook as we were leaving the store. I also gave her some extra money in case we had forgotten anything.

The principal of P.S. 58 invited me to come to the PTA meetings. Marie thought it looked stupid for fathers to attend, but I took off work so I could go. I was always the only man there. Whenever teachers had meetings, the parents donated lunch. I always bought pies and coffee and left them with a note, "From David, Marie, and Charles Rothenberg," but I never told Marie or David.

If I arrived early on the days I picked up David from school, I chatted with the mothers who often asked why I cared so much about my son. "I'm his father. Why not?" was my standard answer. I made it clear to them that David came first with me. I was lonely when I couldn't see him and sent him cards, sometimes with money in them. How I loved my son!

One day David said to me, "Daddy, why can't you live closer to me so I can see you more?" God, how I cried inside myself. I promised to move just as soon as I could. David must have told his mother because Marie called and started verbally hammering away at me again for being around David all the time, but I was not going to allow David's needs to be rejected. No way in hell!

A few weeks later a realtor showed David and me an apartment about seven blocks from where he lived. David loved it, and I immediately put down a deposit. He was eager for me to move in right away but was willing to wait a month so I could fix it up with new furniture and a trunk for his toys. I would do anything for him, and he knew it.

I stayed out of work for a few days to buy the new furniture and move things in little by little. I even bought a Mickey Mouse phone. I wanted it all to be perfect. When everything was set up, Marie and David came over, and they both liked it very much. We went out to dinner, and David stayed with me that night.

For David's birthday I took the day off, made arrangements with Marie to keep him overnight, and surprised him with a trip to the bike store. We bought a big bike with extras like a horn and lights, and since it was too heavy to carry up and down the stairs at Marie's, David's bike stayed at my place. (I wanted to give David a key in case he wanted to ride when I wasn't there, but Marie didn't approve.) David, Marie, and I ate dinner out, and I quietly gave Marie $125 to buy David a birthday present.

Two days later was Father's Day — and my birthday as well. I took David to a neighborhood street festival along with Jimmy, an eight-year-old friend, and his mother. We all enjoyed ourselves and had lots of goodies to eat. This special day was unique to me, a day I'll never forget.

Marie called me one night because her refrigerator broke and she needed help to replace it. I gave her $100 for half the cost of a used refrigerator and then another $100 loan.

I wanted to look for a new job so I could make more money. Sandra Wolfe sent me to a bar on 75th Street, but they didn't have any openings. The bartender, however, suggested that I try Luchow's, which had just moved to 51st and Broadway and was looking for help. I was hired on the spot and started to work the following week. It looked like a gold mine. I had my own station on my first day, and without even knowing the computer system, I served 35 people and earned $75 just for lunch.

I started to give Marie $75 a week now, and every week or two I dropped an extra $25 or $30 in her mailbox. It was for our son, and why not? Everything I did was for David. Marie, too. She is the mother of our boy.

David wanted me to buy a car, and I got a really cute little used one. I gave Marie a set of keys in case she ever wanted to use it. Parking was a problem, but my landlord found a space for me in a nearby lot.

The landlord and his family lived in the apartment below mine. They owned a deli around the corner and all worked very hard — what a nice family. I used to make small improvements in the building, such as installing a lock on the front door and a light in the lobby. I even painted the front door and sometimes cleaned. They worked so many hours, and I wanted to help.

One day at Luchow's the manager heard my beeper go off. When he asked why I was carrying it, I told him that I was divorced and wanted to be available for my son at all times. He thought my devotion was admirable, and he never heard of anyone going that far. Many times the school or Marie would call because David was not feeling well, or he just wanted me to pick him up from school, or Marie needed some money. Mostly, David just wanted to see me. He would always say, "Don't tell Mommy." When it came to my son, I moved quickly. Marie thought I was overdoing my role, but that was her problem.

I used to have a lot of talks with the staff at P.S. 58. They related how David always talked about me and waited for me, and how his face fell if he found out I couldn't pick him up. If I had to work overtime, I would stop by his house and leave a note for him. It was my responsibility to support him and his mother.

I've seen so many fathers fail to pay child support or not see their children — a terrible tragedy! To me, children are the greatest commodity we have in life, and parents should all stand by their children. If a father thinks giving money is his only responsibility, he's a fool. This attitude not only hurts the child, but the mother as well. When arguments start in front of the children, they get nervous and hear things they shouldn't. Children are no dummies; they remember and feel. They are also more forgiving than adults, and more sensitive.

When I showed my affection for David, both publicly and privately, Marie put me down for caring too much. She said, "Fathers don't do this. It's unheard of." But why not? Why couldn't David have and see my love for him? So I never listened when Marie verbally floored me when it came to our son. I could not change myself inside, and I didn't want to. Surely David loved it, and that was the bottom line.

Marie was a hard, hard individual. Though loving, she was always critical and condemning toward others and rarely had nice things to say about anyone. John helped her over the years to cool down. Once when Marie was shouting and calling me all kinds of names on the phone, in the background I heard David say, "Stop yelling at Daddy," and John say, "You shouldn't treat Charles that way. He's a good father." She didn't need to go through a big scene just to get more money; I would have given it to her anyway. Sometimes Marie's mouth tore me apart. She just went after me, but I always walked away. She thought I was a weak person when I did.

In the three years I had custodial problems with Marie — and they were beyond human comprehension, deep and serious — I taped 11 conversations in all and saved them along with my correspondence with attorneys. The four attorneys who heard the tapes were appalled, and they all told me never, never to give up. The adoption request from Marie on January 19, 1981, still comes back to me — how she used John's badge and made it perfectly clear they would both get me one day.

Oktoberfest was a busy time at Luchow's. There was a lot of money to be made, and I put in long hours until the new year. At times I couldn't see David, so I gave Marie money to take him places. Often I got up early to walk him to school. I always called him at night before I started serving dinner, and sometimes David called my beeper as I had a tray held high up in the air. The customers usually smiled when I told them it was my son.

Marie and I went Christmas shopping together again. She had a list a mile long — David wanted an Atari with a new television, plus one for my place. His Aunt Clarissa took him to Bermuda for a week, so I put up $600 extra for the trip, plus expenses. I spent a total of $2,500 for my son, not including $700 I gave Marie for herself. I even bought John a pea coat from David and me and wrapped it with a note thanking him for being nice to my son. I had a ball and loved it. Marie and I wrapped all the presents and hid them in a closet. After I purchased the new TV set, I had $200 left. When I gave it to Marie, she kissed me on the cheek.

I went to Marie's apartment early Christmas morning. We had coffee, and I gave Marie another $100. David got up about 6:00 and was so excited that we had to help him open his presents. I was happy to see our son happy, and we took a few pictures for memories.

I used to go to work thinking how David would talk to me, how he wanted to live with me for a hundred days, then a thousand, how he would raise his arms for me to pick him up, then bite my nose and kiss the hell out of me, saying, "Daddy, I love you!" It was all I wanted to hear every day. David was my life, and I knew all the struggles were worth it.

Friends introduced me to a woman named Anna, and we hit it off immediately. She was a simple person, a separated and working mother of a four-year-old, who lived on Staten Island. Her husband was hot-tempered and violent, and Anna had problems receiving support from him. I helped her out with money, loaned her my car, and bought some things she needed. Usually I don't take that quickly to a woman, but Anna was different. She was old-fashioned and down-to-earth — something I couldn't pinpoint, but it was there for both of us. Unfortunately, our relationship ended because of a tragedy — not Anna's, but my son — that reached worldwide attention.

VII

Early in January 1983 when I reported for work at Luchow's, the manager told me I was laid off, pending an investigation of some employees who were suspected of using a master computer key to steal money from the restaurant. The computer company claimed to have received a check from me to purchase the key. I was completely stunned — I mean stunned! The maitre d' thought I had nothing to do with it and told me that a recently fired employee was the main suspect. Nonetheless, Luchow's had to investigate before I could be called back.

I was worried about how I would support my son, for although I had saved a lot of money, it goes fast when one is unemployed. I wanted to see the check with my name on it, but I couldn't get a copy of the forgery. I knew I did not do it and wondered who would put my name on a check. Or was it all a set-up? I worked so hard at Luchow's, coming in early every day and cleaning up after dirty waiters. It was a habit of mine, not only at Luchow's but at all my other jobs.

I took a job as a driver for the Battery Car Service on Court Street, using my own car. It was good money and in my own neighborhood, and at the same time I applied for unemployment insurance for the first time in my life. Luchow's wrote that I was suspected of stealing from the restaurant, but since I was not indicted and had been fired, I was eligible for benefits. They felt something was very fishy about all this.

Once again I sought legal advice from Wayne Price. He felt that because I had a criminal record, the cops were trying to use me, close their books, and lock me up. He told me to fight and that he would represent me if needed.

Several days later I received a call from Detective Harry Hard, who informed me that Luchow's had been broken into on January 14, 1983, and he wanted to talk to me. When I got over my shock, I realized that I had been in Raleigh, North Carolina, visiting Carol Henderson from January 12 to January 17. I wasn't even in New York, and I told Detective Hard that I couldn't possibly be responsible. Detective Hard said he would investigate further and call me back.

I consulted Wayne Price and showed him proof of the dates of my trip. I also told him that I called Marie from Carol's on January 16. He said not to worry.

Two weeks passed, and I had a message on my answering machine from Detective Hard's partner, Detective Johnson. When I returned his call, he threatened that he and his partner would come and get me if I didn't turn myself in for questioning. This time I made a formal complaint with the police because of the threats and advised Wayne Price of what was happening.

Detective Hard informed Wayne that he was going to charge me with the crime at Luchow's and demanded that I come in. Wayne encouraged me to turn myself in and promised to get me out on bail immediately. He advised me that the police can arrest anyone as a suspect, and the only way to clear up this whole thing was for me to go in. I agreed to a time on February 26, 1983, two days later, and gave

Wayne my bank book and power of attorney to take money out for my bail and fees.

I was mad as hell now, for Wayne knew I was in North Carolina and did not commit the robbery at Luchow's. He was mad, too, and was ready to move quickly after I turned myself in. I couldn't believe what was going on. The whole thing was just madness.

David and I spent the evening together. After I took him home, I just drove around thinking about what had happened to me. My life was being turned around, only because I had a criminal record and the cops wanted to close their books — baloney!

When I got home, there was a another threatening message waiting for me from Detective Hard who said, "If you don't come in now, we'll come and get you." This upset me tremendously. I had had it! I couldn't take it anymore!

I decided not to turn myself in and instead to take David away for a vacation, one that was long overdue ever since the Florida vacation I had planned in 1981 that Marie denied me. I wrote Wayne Price a letter, informing him that I was not turning myself in and I wanted these cops to leave me alone. I wrote that I was going upstate so that when I didn't show up at the police station, they wouldn't know where to find me. And my decision was final!

I made arrangements to move into the YMCA on 9th Street in Brooklyn when I returned from vacation, and I had to vacate my apartment as quickly as possible, leaving much behind. My life, for the time being, was ruined, and I would have to start all over again. I was even willing to take a lie detector test, but they said no.

One day remained before I had to turn myself in, and I still had a lot of thinking to do. I took long walks and tried to figure out so many things: why Marie and John always went after me, why they were both so involved with themselves instead of realizing David's needs, why I continued to get verbal abuse from Marie. Why did I have to suffer emotionally because of Marie's hard, sandpaper personality that I could never stop, try as I might? I wondered why people in general never stopped and thought about the reasons they dream, feel, cry, love, hate, condemn others, think only of themselves, not sharing or caring about others' feelings. I wondered why Marie was always attacking me with her mouth in front of our son and John, and even in front of her friends and family. I wondered why Marie liked to tell people I was a criminal, why she seemed to enjoy hurting people, and why she laughed at me when I reached out to others. These things, and so many more, bothered me for years, but I never showed it or voiced my anger or opinions. I always walked away!

I picked up my bank book from Wayne Price's office, making up an excuse about needing some money. I wanted to be with my son for a week and let David be with his father. I knew David would like a vacation — a surprise to him. Marie gave me permission to take him for a week, but I didn't tell her my plans. It was a good time because she wanted to spend time with John and, according to her, get David out of her hair for awhile.

We packed a big blue duffle bag with everything David would need for a week, and I took him to Helen's Restaurant for dinner. I hadn't told him that I had arranged for Anna and her daughter and sister to join us, and he ran out of the restaurant crying. I knew then that he only wanted to be with me.

Well, I had to bribe David with a few dollars to play the arcade, and he agreed to eat after he played. I told him that I thought he was just like his mother at times and that he must learn to listen to me. About 30 minutes later David had his meal with us, and we all went to Staten Island for the night. When we were alone, I asked David if he wanted to go to Disneyland. I had already purchased the tickets, and when I showed them to David, he threw his arms around me and told me he loved me and wanted to stay with me all the time. Now he was happy!

Anna asked us to stay over, but after David played with her daughter and sister for a time, he wanted to leave. Anna knew I was going to take David on vacation; I had, in fact, confided in her about John and Marie on many occasions. Anna thought David should be with me for a while. She knew how much I loved and fought for my son, and we used to discuss for hours how important it was that David have all the benefits of a father's love at his tender age.

Before we left, I gave Anna a few hundred dollars. She was broke, and I felt bad and wanted to assist her. Anna was a gem and didn't take advantage of me. She had never met anyone like me before and thought I was too kind, but I told her I'd always been that way and there was no need to say thank you. I hugged and kissed them all good-bye, and David and I spent the night at a Holiday Inn. David was as happy as a bee. He kept putting his arms around me, saying, "We're going to Disneyland, Daddy. I love you."

Because of the cops and the temporary ruin of my life from a false accusation, I withdrew all my money from the bank and sold my car. I remembered our phone conversations and knew the cops were going to get a warrant to search my apartment. These guys were no good and didn't want to listen to the truth. The pressure was on, and they only wanted to close the case. I was the scapegoat.

I thought back over the years to when David when born, how I sold one of my laundromats just so he and Marie could have all those things, how I didn't see him for two years when I was in prison and heard from Marie only a few times, how I couldn't take him to church on Sundays because Marie wouldn't let me. (We did go once for Bible study, and we also put some money in the box and lighted a candle.)

I thought about so many other unnecessary problems with Marie and John; it was terrible. I looked back all those years — the fatherly struggles, the threats I had from Marie, the thousands of dollars I spent on attorneys — and wondered why Marie was like that. All I wanted was to be David's father. I could never figure out why Marie came down on me so hard and wondered if what she said about me was just a product of herself. It all bothered me for years, yet I never showed or expressed it much. I kept it all within.

I thought about my taped conversations with Marie. I realized it was not me she was really talking about, but herself, her personality, her beliefs. When I reread all the letters to and from the attorneys, me, Marie, and John, I wondered why this had to happen. We're all human beings, and there must have been a way to work it out. But Marie always plugged her ears and walked away. And she had John beside her. John was her protection, but from what? Not me. Marie and John were planning their future, forgetting David's needs, and they took life with a grain of salt. Even Marie's sisters said they couldn't control Marie's mouth. I know that on many occasions hate is love, and people express themselves in a negative way only when something happens to them that doesn't make their day. They take it out on someone else, not meaning it and often having to apologize for their actions and feeling guilty. ■

Analysis II
Jack Wilson

Around the time of his marriage, Charles' contacts with religion appear to have waned. When he finally married Marie, he was content to be married before a Justice of the Peace instead of seeking out the church. Charles doesn't tell us why: perhaps he simply felt distanced from Christianity at that point in his life, or perhaps he didn't perceive the church as anything more than an institution to provide solutions to his problems as he presented them.

Similarly, Charles did not seek to have David baptized for several months after his birth. He did ask Father Duffy (now Bishop Duffy) to come to his home and bless David, but he evidences no theological understanding of these rites. Charles was involved in purchasing a laundromat at the time, and David's baptism and blessing seem to be little more than an attempt to get things in order at the start of his new business venture.

Charles' shallow conscience and his ability to subordinate any sense of wrongdoing to meet his needs for esteem and belonging remain evident into this period of his life. His mother-in-law became seriously ill at the same time he was experiencing business setbacks. On an impulse he forged a check for $29,000. He does admit that he knew forgery was wrong, but this knowledge didn't hinder him in any way from carrying out his plan over a period of several days. He knew his mother-in-law needed help, and he was determined to provide it by giving her doctor $3,000. Perhaps Charles believed he could in some way buy a cure for his mother-in-law and save the day, so to speak. He gives no indication of offering prayers for her, and the whole episode once again backfired. He claims that this crime precipitated his divorce.

During his subsequent incarceration at the Clinton Correctional Facility, Charles apparently became active once again in religious pursuits. He writes that he became very close to the Catholic priest and to God, and that he knew everything would be okay, all in the same breath. We have to understand these statements as a general sense of religious well-being that periodically prevailed in his life. But again, Charles offers no written evidence that he felt guilty for his crime. He gives the impression of one who has a diminished sense of right and wrong, reducing the motivation for the crime simply to love of the dollar bill and a desire to help people.

Once again, Bishop Duffy came to his aid and enabled Charles to find housing upon his release. Charles' behavior fell into a well-established pattern: he would go on without any religious pursuits beyond the occasional prayer or visit to a church or pastor until he got into serious trouble. Then as a last resort, he would turn to the church or some religious leader for assistance. He was, apparently, never turned away. This acceptance had the potential of reinforcing to Charles something of the free grace of God. But it also potentially reinforced a shallow concept of sin.

Charles' description of his relationship with David also reveals his own weak conscience and lack of sense of authority, as well as his needs for self-esteem and belonging. In spite of Charles' statement that he had a normal upbringing, his concept of a loving father is that of the proverbial "sugar daddy." He had no sense of the instruction given in both Old and New Testaments concerning parental roles.[4] He evidences little, if any, awareness of his responsibility as David's father to influence the development of David's character and no sense of parental authority.

Charles seems to define love for David first in terms of economics and then in terms of displays of affection. He takes great joy in recounting all of his gifts to David, the extra money that he gave to Marie, and the attention that he lavished on David. He relates spending $2,500 on David for Christmas in 1982 so that David could have *"everything he wanted."* On one occasion he took David to a restaurant, and David didn't want to eat. Charles' solution was to bribe David with money to play the arcade, and later that evening, Charles offered to take him to Disneyland. Charles comment on David's reaction was, *"Now he was happy!"*

In all of the descriptions of his interaction with David, Charles places very little emphasis on religion, which is intriguing in view of Charles' own positive relationships with the church and religious leaders. Perhaps he felt that David didn't need the church in the same way that he did; as David's father, he could provide the kinds of experiences that would make David feel loved and happy. Since it appears that for Charles religion was primarily a source for such experiences, he probably felt little need to press any religious issues with David. ∎

---

[4] Such as the Fifth in the Ten Commandments, or as appears in Ephesians 6:1-4.

▨▨▨▨ Andrew Savicky

By now, Charles' behavior patterns are familiar. He acted out of the low self-esteem and abandonment of childhood, allowing himself little happiness and always turning good into bad. He seldom asserted himself and preferred to depend passively on others. His need for approval and acceptance led him to do things for others, causing them to feel somehow obligated to him.

Despite their divorce, Marie still occupied a very important place in Charles' life. While he was still in jail, she could minimize contact with him by seldom answering his letters. Once released, however, he was impossible to ignore. Charles even asked her to meet him at the bus station and put him up for a few days as if she were somehow responsible for his welfare.

It is likely that Charles was looking for his mother in his relationship with Marie. She seemed to fulfill his need for pain: he called her *"coarse,"* *"critical,"* *"condemning,"* and said she would *"dig her mouth"* at him. He writes of Marie *"going after [him] with her mouth"* and causing him to *"feel less than human."* Yet Charles didn't try to stop her, for to stop her would relieve his pain. Time and time again, he hid his own feelings and just walked away from her verbal abuse. Nonetheless, he worked at maintaining this unhealthy relationship. In fact, the more abuse he received from Marie, the more he tried to do for her and David. Perhaps her abuse was acceptable because it meant that she still cared about him.

Almost immediately he started giving money to Marie in an attempt to buy her affection and good will. A lesson Charles had learned from his mother was to pay to get what he wanted, and he applied this lesson to his life. He says that *"the buck"* always made Marie happy, and he used it to obtain her attention and approval as well as his ultimate needs and desires. Anytime he wanted something from Marie (to take a day off work, go shopping with him, go to a Broadway show, see David), he paid her and at the same time placed her under an obligation to him. He may have been buying her good will, but he certainly expected something in return.

Money also played a large part in his relationship with David, starting with the expensive toy Charles bought to give David after his release from jail. He spent extravagantly for David's Christmas and birthday gifts and moved to a different apartment and bought new furniture in an effort please him. He even bought off David's bad behavior when he bribed David with money for the arcade to get him to eat his dinner one night. Needing their recognition and approval, Charles made something of a ceremony of announcing to Marie and David that he would be responsible for all of David's expenses. Charles was giving David all the material things he never had himself, but he failed to give him a good example to live by. He was also buying ownership and control.

David was the focus of an enormous amount of Charles' energies. He claims he worked long hours to support David, to buy him everything he wanted and needed. Perhaps he was overindulgent because he felt guilty for not being there for David. He purchased an answering machine so he could receive David's messages and then a beeper so that he could be in touch with David immediately. Charles tells of kisses and hugs and I-love-yous and of trying to supply to David everything he had lacked in his own childhood, but what is missing in the narrative is any sense of real communication between father and son and a right example for David to live by. He may have set out to be for David the father Charles never had, but, of course, he had no role model. Afraid of losing his son, he tried to bind David to him by obligation.

Marie's relationship to John was clearly a threat to Charles. Unable to end his dependence on his relationship with Marie, Charles was afraid John would displace him there as well as in David's life. This fear was confirmed when Marie asked Charles to allow John to adopt David, a request that caused Charles a great deal of anger and anguish. Not only did Marie put him down by comparing him unfavorably to John, reports Charles, but she suggested that David would forget him. David was so important to Charles that he even stepped out of character and confronted John on the adoption issue. (This confrontation demonstrates some potential for success in therapy.) But for the most part, Charles continued his passive dependent behavior in relating to John and, back in character, even bought him an expensive Christmas present to dissipate the hostility.

Charles enjoyed the noble and heroic role he assumed as David's father. Walking David to school, attending PTA meetings, purchasing refreshments for the teachers, being the "victim" in a scene with Marie and John in front of the school, helping his landlord — these were all circumstances in which people were obligated to like and support Charles.

His dependent personality was particularly evident at this time as Charles cast about for someone to solve his problems for him, someone to be his missing parent. Unwilling or unable to deal with Marie's "mouth" himself, he went to several lawyers to intercede for him. And he came to depend upon Roy Cohn's secretary who suggested job opportunities and listened to his troubles. Charles never discovered that he could take the initiative for his own success.

Charles seems to have been unaware of the extent of his antisocial behavior. Having no role model for honesty, he was often dishonest in "small" ways. He thought nothing of calling in sick to work if he made other plans; he taped his conversations with Marie; after his firing from Luchow's, he collected unemployment compensation even though he had a new job. His criminal behavior he blamed on his desire to help other people, relieving himself of responsibility. Whether or not Charles committed the crime at Luchow's is unclear. Charles, of course, denied it, but why then was he so afraid of turning himself in for questioning? It was his inability to deal with this situation that led directly to his trip to California and its disastrous results.

Unable to sort out his emotions, Charles says, *"I know that on many occasions hate is love and people express themselves in a negative way only when something happens to them that doesn't make their day."* In his confusion he no doubt thought of his mother's abuse (hate) as love, of Marie's hateful remarks as love; and Charles expressed himself with hate when he thought he was expressing love. Perhaps it was all he knew. ■

Charles Rothenberg
Tragedy

I

The next morning — February 26, 1983, the day I was supposed to turn myself in to the police — David and I boarded the plane for California. He was very tired and slept in my arms. When we reached our destination, we picked up our baggage, took a cab to the Holiday Inn in Buena Park, and checked in.

The first thing David noticed at the hotel was the arcade. He asked me for quarters and started to play. It was a good thing because it was raining hard. David played for quite a while — we played some of the games together — and ate in the coffee shop when we got hungry. How David loved to sit across from me and eat his hamburgers, french fries, coke, and ice cream. He returned to the games until he got tired, and then we went to our room to sleep.

In the morning it was still raining. The car rental office was not open yet, so David and I took the hotel's free bus to Disneyland. (The bus driver told me that Disneyland never closes.) We took a train that passed every section of the park. In spite of the rain, David wanted to go on a boat that passed kind of an underground, a beautiful spectacle that we enjoyed. He wanted to go on more rides, but it was raining so hard that he finally said, "Daddy, let's go and play the arcade at the hotel."

On the way, we stopped at a wax museum. David and I both loved it there. Every character looked real. This place was so beautiful that we came back three times.

It was still quite early, and the rain stopped. We returned to Disneyland and enjoyed whatever David wanted to do. But we weren't there long before the rains came again, and this time it poured! We waited a long time for the bus to the hotel, but it didn't come. We were both drenched and made our way to one of the buildings to wait. I started to worry that David would get sick. As I was asking for information about getting back to the hotel, an elderly couple offered to drive us. We jumped at the chance and were grateful to them.

We both changed into dry clothes and then went to the arcade. It was a blessing that the hotel offered this amusement, as I wasn't sure what David would have done otherwise. While David was playing, I rented a car for the week and picked up information about things to do that I thought David might enjoy.

Late in the afternoon, we went to a nearby health club and signed up for the minimum two-week membership. When David saw all the activities available, this was the place where he wanted to stay. We had a wonderful time and used all the facilities — swimming pool, sauna, tennis courts, weight-lifting and exercise equipment. People watched us and smiled all the time we were there. I guess not many parents brought their children here, and they thought we were amusing. I applauded David for every achievement, every effort, and rewarded him with "I love you!" As usual, I showed it.

After dinner we found a bowling alley. David loved to bowl, and he was pretty good, too. I let him play himself out until he got tired. Before we went back to our room, I checked at a travel agency to see if we could get reservations for Disney World in Florida, but they were totally booked. I felt so bad that I hadn't checked the weather before leaving New York, but we came suddenly and I didn't think to do it. Still, David was still having a good time and said so many times, "Daddy, I love you, I love you."

We awoke the next morning, hoping to find that the rain had stopped, but it was still pouring. We spent the day at the arcade, the bowling alley, the wax museum, and the health club. We were both as tired as hell by the end.

I remember David most of the day telling me how much he loved me, wishing I could come back home with Mommy, then wanting to stay in California, then wanting to move in with me in Brooklyn — a normal kid's thinking. I loved my son so much, and sometimes it hurt me to hear his thoughts. He was very sensitive and often expressed his emotions more through his actions than his words. I knew when David wanted to be with me, either by his look, stretching out his arms to me, sending me a valentine, or just calling my machine to say "I love you."

Even Marie told me that David loved me, but she and John had other plans. Marie told me that when she married John, they would be living in Long Island and it would be up to me to get out there to see David — but only if she and John let me. She was always negative about me and other people. Her motto was "the hell with other people."

David and I got up that Monday morning — March 1, 1983 — and ate breakfast. Again it was raining hard, but David didn't care because he wanted to play in the arcade.

I called Marie to tell her I'd return David on March 5th. She asked me, "Where is my son, Charles? Do you know the police are after you? Where are you, Charles?"

I answered, "I'm on a short vacation with David, and we'll return on the 5th."

Marie then started to tell me about Luchow's. I told her that I had nothing to do with it, but she said, "Why don't you turn yourself in?"

"Because I didn't do it," I repeated.

Marie went on to talk about John, how he was going to get me, and said that when I did return with David, I'd never see him again. She told me to leave David at the day care center, but since it would be closed on Saturday, I said I'd take him to her place.

Marie kept telling me that she hated me and would make sure that I'd never, never see my son again. She brought up John's name again and used his profession and badge as she always did.

Before I hung up, I reiterated that I would return on the 5th and would take David to her apartment. She said again, and this time very forcefully, "Charles, I will make sure you never see David again when you return."

I knew she meant what she said.

I was a bit nervous, not only because of this conversation but also because of the Luchow's incident. For the first time, Marie scared me. I always walked away from her verbal attacks against me, but this time something inside me said that she really meant it.

What Marie did not know was that I taped the entire call. I always taped our conversations from the day she asked me to give David up for adoption. I guess that proposal never went away from me. I always seemed to go back to that day at the coffee shop — a vicious request. It bothered me!

I sat in the lobby and played back the conversation at least ten times. Marie bothered me today, yesterday, and all the years I've known her — but only her mouth. She never knew when to stop and zip it up. I decided to mail this tape and three others to an attorney in New York to hold for me.

I was not feeling very well emotionally, but I didn't show it to David. My thoughts were on that conversation. David was all over me, telling me how much he loved me. We had a wonderful day. We did whatever he wanted — bowling, the health club, the arcade.

I was deeply disturbed and couldn't get that call out of my mind. I'm not sure what really hit me, but I wanted to end it all, to leave Marie in her misery with John. I was ready, in some way, to commit suicide with David, to end it all, to get away from Marie's mouth and the years of verbal abuse that I could never understand. I thought about the phone call, the adoption issue, the constant threats over the years, and wondered why I was always her target. I could never figure it out, but it had to end. I guess it finally got to me. I knew I couldn't take it any longer.

On our way back to the hotel that night, something hit me all of a sudden when I saw a sign reading: Travelodge — water beds. I'm not exactly sure what the hell was going on in my head, but I knew I wanted David and me to die somewhere, somehow, so Marie and John could suffer not ever knowing what happened to us. On an impulse I asked David if he felt like sleeping on a water bed. He was delighted, and I reserved a room for one night. Then we went back to the Holiday Inn.

The rain continued to fall on March 2nd, so we took off again for the wax museum, bowling, and the health club. I picked David up at times, holding him tightly. I was so emotionally drained over Marie's threat that I just wanted to be with my son.

In my mind that day, I tried to figure out how, where, and when David and I could die together. I first thought about Niagara Falls, just jumping with David into the water. I was all confused! I thought about sleeping pills for both of us and bought an over-the-counter drug at a pharmacy, but it wouldn't be fast enough. Then I thought about fire. That would probably be the quickest way if we both were asleep after taking sleeping pills. I wasn't sure. I was all mixed up and confused.

I purchased a can of kerosene at a hardware store. I wasn't sure what I was looking for, but this was the one I decided on. I took it to the Travelodge, where I placed it in a cubbyhole under the sink.

Back at the Holiday Inn, David played the arcade while I sat in the lobby thinking. I was going through a lot in my mind — the years of verbal torment and abuse from Marie, the adoption issue, her threat to keep David from me — and for the first time it was real to me. I thought about how David and I would die while we were sleeping. The pills were not enough, and I'm not even sure if I actually gave David any. I took some sleeping pills because I wanted to relax. I was very upset and nervous. I wanted to die. I couldn't take Marie's mouth any longer.

David and I went to the Travelodge about 8:00 p.m. We both undressed and started to watch television. David finally went to sleep. I got to thinking again about the phone call, the adoption issue, the years I could not zipper Marie's mouth — you name it, and I was thinking about it. I was very angry, but not at my son. It was Marie, her mouth. It never seemed to close. She never wanted it to. She enjoyed hurting me, especially with John. He was her protection.

I remember waking up about 10:30. I looked over at my son and kissed him and kissed him so many times. I turned the TV off and got out the kerosene, pouring it all over the place until the white can was empty. I stepped outside and put the empty can in a trash barrel that was near the car. I went back in and looked at my son. I kissed him a few more times and again started to think about my conversation with Marie, and I played it back like all those other conversations. I was very angry, furious at Marie and John. I did nothing to them, only provide for my son. They were both uncomfortable because I had to be around.

In my mind I didn't want to hurt my son. I was not angry with him. He surely was not to blame. I just wanted to zipper Marie's mouth — that's all.

I turned to my son, kissed him, and decided to wait till another time — maybe never — I was not sure. I loved David so much, and at that moment, giving him one more kiss, I decided not to go through with it. I went back to sleep.

II

Suddenly, I was out the door with a shadow of flames in front of me. I'm not sure, really. For a few seconds — maybe longer, I don't know — I saw flames in front of me and thought the world was coming to an end. For that few seconds out the door, Marie's mouth was on my mind, that phone call — sudden flashes coming back at me over the years with her — and I realized my son was in the room. I realized I had a match in my hand and saw the flames in the room, and for a moment I tried to go back in to get my son. But then I panicked and ran to the car. I was scared!

I remember getting into the car with my left leg burning and some smoke coming out of my pants. I pressed a towel that was on the front seat hard on the area around my ankle. It was raining so hard. To be perfectly honest, I was not sure if my car was facing the hotel room or the reverse. I was thinking of my son and rolled out of the driveway at about 40 miles per hour. I saw someone in front of me and thought I almost hit the person; but as I was driving out of the area, no one was there.

I was so angry with Marie — that phone call, those years she verbally abused me — that I couldn't think at all. I was crying a lot and couldn't see too well to drive. I heard fire engines, and as I was driving slowly around, I saw them go into the Travelodge. I got very nervous. I wanted to be with my son, but I was scared. I didn't know what to do. An ambulance turned into the Travelodge, and within minutes, it went back out. I knew my son was in it. I was so scared! I went to a restaurant a few blocks away and drank a cup of coffee, still crying. The waitress asked me if I was okay, but I didn't answer. I immediately paid and left. I was so scared!

I checked into a Quality Inn a few blocks from the fire and called every hospital in the area. No one in the emergency rooms heard of a child coming in. I asked an operator how I could find a hospital that took someone who had been burned, and she gave me a few numbers. I called five or six more hospitals and finally spoke with a nurse who told me of a child who had come in badly burned and was sent to the University of California/Irvine Medical Center Burn Unit. When I reached the UCI Burn Unit, a nurse told me that a boy was just brought in with third degree burns and in critical condition. She said it was very bad and it looked as if he would die.

Crying and scared, I didn't know what to do. My mind was still on Marie's mouth, and I was still angry with her. I couldn't figure out how I got out the door at the Travelodge without knowing it. It was impossible! I wanted to see my son and be next to him. I didn't know what to do.

I kept calling the Burn Unit, and after a while they seemed to recognize my voice. When they started asking me questions, I hung up. I packed up all my belongings at the Holiday Inn and went back to the Quality Inn. I kept calling to see how David was, but they didn't even know his name, they told me.

I was so nervous now. I knew I had done a very bad thing. I took my anger out on my son, an anger I never knew before, an anger I never thought would come to this. I knew David might die. I was scared and didn't know what to do or whom to turn to.

I decided to go to San Francisco under a false name, and I picked "David Love." I was so nervous and upset about what I had done. I wasn't even sure if they knew I did it. I just didn't know.

I registered at the YMCA as David Love, but because I didn't want to show my true identification, I could stay only one night. I kept calling the UCI Burn Unit to find out about my son, but no one would give me any details. I couldn't sleep and walked for hours thinking about Marie and John. I didn't want to hurt anyone, especially my son. I only wanted to shut Marie's mouth. I was so upset!

The next day I moved into the Monroe Residence where they didn't require any ID. One of the nurses had told me that Sergeant Dick Hafdahl was in charge of the case, and I called him at the Buena Park Police Department. (I kept on calling Sergeant Hafdahl like he was someone I had known for many years, but I still didn't give him my name.) He wanted to know who I was, if I had anything to do with the fire, and if I knew the child. He asked me the child's name. I said I didn't know but wanted to know how he was. He replied that the child had third degree burns and was not expected to live.

That information prompted me to send Marie a telegram — I didn't want David to be alone! In my message I told Marie that she had done enough to me, that I couldn't take it anymore and wanted to end my life. I included the phone numbers of the Burn Unit and Sergeant Hafdahl. I tried to call Sergeant Hafdahl again, but he wasn't in. The hospital informed me that David was still alive.

I went to a clothing store to buy a few things I needed. After I gave the clerk my American Express card, he stayed on the phone a long time. Something inside me said, "Get out of this place." When I offered to pay cash instead, the clerk still tried to detain me; but I gave him the money and left quickly. As I walked down the street, I looked back to see a police car stopping in front of the store. I walked very slowly to the corner without being noticed, and when I turned to go to the Residence, several police cars were surrounding that building. I found a phone booth and called the Residence. Pretending to be a police officer, I found out from the switchboard operator that the police were looking for me.

Marie must have already received my telegram, and, in turn, she had probably called the Buena Park Police Department. I was never sure how the police found out I was living at the Monroe Residence, but I guess I told the clerk at the clothing store. The entire block was surrounded, and I was nervous. I walked down the street and purchased things I needed at Woolworth's. Then I checked into the YMCA. Next I cashed all my travelers checks at various banks. I called Sergeant Hafdahl again, and this time he knew who I was. I was so scared and only wanted to know about David. I didn't know what to do.

I called my friend, Bishop Duffy. We talked for a while, but I didn't tell him what had happened, only that I had moved to California. I just wanted to hear his voice. I was lonely, scared, and very confused. I kept calling the hospital and Sergeant Hafdahl. For six days I never slept.

When I talked to Sergeant Hafdahl on March 9, 1983, he asked me to give myself up. He told me to call him back on a different number so our call wouldn't be recorded, and I did. But after we talked for a while, I noticed a click on the phone, and I hung up. I was just so tired. I only had David on my mind now.

I picked up a sandwich, then returned to the YMCA. As I walked through the door, many police officers jumped me from behind. One officer searched me from head to foot, handcuffed me, and placed me against a wall. He held a photo of me and said, "It's all over, Charles."

III

I was very scared and started to cry. I was escorted to a car and placed in the back with an officer on each side. They tried to calm me down. One said, "You should have done this to your wife." When I looked at him in shock, he added, "I don't think you meant to hurt your son. I think you meant to do it to your wife."

Many cameras awaited us at the police station. I didn't expect this, but I said nothing. Sergeant Hafdahl and Detective Flanigan flew in from Orange County. I recognized Sergeant Hafdahl's voice immediately and of course asked how my son was. He said, "Okay so far." I told him that I had $13,000 in cash in my room at the YMCA and asked him to give it to my son and Marie. I didn't have much else in that room except a folder containing about 75 pictures of my son, his mother, and all of us together. I hoped they would be safe with my property.

Two officers drove me back to Orange County in a van. They were very nice and talked to me most of the way when I was crying. All I could think about was my son. I was just so drained mentally.

We arrived at the Orange County Sheriff's Office, and a crowd of reporters were waiting as I stepped off the van with my hands and legs shackled. They kept shouting questions at me on my way to the building.

Sergeant Hafdahl, Detective Flanigan, and the district attorney were waiting for me in a conference room. They said they wanted to talk to me about the fire, gave me my rights, and asked if I wanted an attorney present. I said no. I was sitting at the foot of the table in front of a glass panel, and I suspected that the interview was being videotaped. I told them what I knew and remembered of "that day" and kept asking how my son was. After about two hours I was taken to the Orange County Jail.

I was in a cell by myself, under observation, because of the publicity and notoriety. All of a sudden I was alone with no one to talk to and no way to get information about my son. I was scared and couldn't sleep.

A number of days passed, and I had heard nothing. One morning a newspaper was slipped under my door with the front page featuring a picture of my son (one I had taken when he was younger) and a story about the fire and my boy's condition. He was still fighting to survive with many complications still to be overcome. An officer told me they would give me any information coming in about my son to help me cope.

Chris Dee, a reporter from the Orange County Register, came to see me. I accepted the interview only to see how my son was. If anyone knew, it would be a reporter. I was escorted to a booth were we could talk in a noncontact visit by phone, looking through a glass at each other. Chris told me he had seen me in court and advised me that David was still alive and that his mother and John Cirillo were there. He said he thought something was wrong with this case and wanted to hear my story. I agreed to talk with him only if he would keep me totally informed on my son's medical progress.

We talked for two days about my life, my mother, my son, Bishop Duffy, Marie, John — whatever he wanted to learn about me. Chris was young but seemed very honest and professional. He said that my son's tragedy had reached national attention and his paper wanted to know the other side, which would be on the front page the next day.

I also talked with Nancy Wride, a reporter from the Los Angeles Times, who waited four hours to see me. She asked me about the case and wanted as much information as possible. She was honest with me and did not pull any punches.

The next morning, March 25, 1983, a newspaper was put under my door with the headline "Charles Rothenberg offers his body to his son." I was shocked because, although I had made that statement to Chris and Nancy, I didn't think they'd print it. They reported everything I told them with very little editing. They seemed to want both sides of the story and must have thought whatever I gave them was important.

The Register and Times articles about me were decent, fair, and objective. I found these reporters to be interested in my son, and for this reason I spoke only to Nancy and Chris. I declined other interviews because the situation was getting out of hand, exploiting me and my son.

(Later Larry Nathanson, a reporter for the New York Post, wrote me a letter requesting my side of the story. He promised he'd send me the article and any future articles on my son. I decided to write to him, not to discuss the case but to try to reach my son through him. I knew Marie would probably not allow our son to know what I had to say, but I gave it a shot. A week later Larry Nathanson answered my letter and wrote a decent article. He told me that he had heard many good things about me from employers and neighbors in Brooklyn and that he felt I didn't want to hurt my son. He made it clear that the only negative comments were from my ex-wife, and he thought she was using the publicity and my son's condition to justify her role.)

Ramon Ortiz, an attorney from the Orange County Public Defender's Office, came to see me and announced that he was going to be my lawyer. I was not comfortable with him at all — he seemed "cool" and manipulative, and he called me "Chuck." In our conversation he focused on the reporters and the publicity, not on my son. He told me that every newspaper in the country had picked up this case because it was so unusual and the world was watching. He admonished me for speaking with the reporters and declared that any further contact from them should be forwarded to him. I advised Mr. Ortiz that if he was only interested in going to Hollywood, he should send me another lawyer — my only concern was with my son. He backed off and said I could talk to reporters as long as I didn't discuss the case. I retorted that I had no plans to discuss the case, but I would go out of my way to get information about my son. My instincts told me that he was only in this for the publicity, and I didn't like his attitude at all. Mr. Ortiz said he would come back the next day to get to know me better.

Later that same day I was told I had a visitor from Whittier, California, named Joyce Chapman. I was still in a bad mood from talking with Mr. Ortiz; nonetheless, I accepted the visit. When I reached the visiting room, a thin, tired-looking woman was waiting for me. She told me she had read my story in the newspapers and had waited for me for ten hours, praying that I would see her. She said she was moved by my story and wanted to be my friend.

Joyce told me about her family — her husband, Phil, and her two boys, Sean and David — and that all of them were Christians. I grew suspicious and hoped she wouldn't shove God in my face, like some already had done since the tragedy. But Joyce was different. She just spoke about Jesus. I felt she was at peace with herself and came to me as a concerned mother who wanted to be my friend. She promised to visit again and to keep me informed about anything she heard about my son.

As promised, Mr. Ortiz came back the next day. I hadn't slept and was thinking about my boy and what to do. The whole thing frightened me. I told Mr. Ortiz that I didn't want to have a preliminary hearing. He was shocked and said he was sure that the judge would never allow it. I was adamant and instructed him to ask for a waiver, giving up all my rights for my son's sake and so Marie could stay by his bedside. I was not concerned about myself, but about my boy and his needs.

Mr. Ortiz seemed to enjoy his role as my attorney. He wanted to go to trial and go after Marie and John. He told me he had letters from attorneys as evidence that Marie had lied when she said we had no custody dispute, and he wanted to expose her. I demanded that he turn those letters over to me and never use them. It took me a long time to convince him, but exposing Marie would serve no purpose. I made this decision because David needed his mother, and David was the bottom line.

IV

Mr. Ortiz and I walked into Judge Dave Back's courtroom on the day the preliminary hearing was scheduled. He was still trying to change my mind. I had wanted to plead guilty from the beginning, but Mr. Ortiz was the one holding off. Now he would listen to me, or I would fire him! I was getting tired of reports from Chris Dee and Joyce Chapman that Mr. Ortiz was making statements to the press and using this case for his own purposes.

At the proper time, he informed Judge Back that I wanted to forego my preliminary hearing so that Marie could stay at my son's bedside. I was furious that Tom Avdeef, the district attorney, had asked Marie to be present and that she had left our son, still in critical condition, at the hospital. I never thought she would leave him, but she did. Marie loved to hurt people emotionally — especially me — and now that I had burned my own son, she was taking every opportunity to use David's condition and the entire situation to get back at me. I knew that because I knew her! She thought I was weak because I always walked away from her mouth.

The district attorney asked me if I really knew what I was doing in asking for the preliminary hearing to end. I just said yes. He said he had no objections. I was relieved that Marie could go back to David's bedside where she should have been.

The judge stated that hardly one defendant a year opts to forego a preliminary hearing, but I did not want my son to be without his mother. I was guilty, and I didn't want Mr. Ortiz to go to trial just to expose Marie. What sense would it make? None!

Mr. Ortiz and the district attorney were making a mockery of this case and, on many occasions, so was Marie. I finally put a stop to it, but only by many arguments with my attorney. He just didn't give a damn about my son or my feelings. He never wanted to talk about what I felt. He and Mr. Avdeef just put on their individual acts for the reporters.

Judge Luis Cardenas signed an order for me to give blood to my son, but the order was not carried out. Officers at the jail offered to donate their time to take me to the UCI Medical Center, but Mr. Ortiz was concerned only about himself and the publicity he was getting. So because of him, the blood was never given. He never gave the signed order to the Orange County Jail.

Chris Dee told me he heard a rumor that I would visit my son, probably started when Mr. Ortiz talked to reporters after I gave him a New York Post article with the headline, "Father may go to visit his son if he keeps pining for his dad." I was really upset that he was looking for more headlines, but I wanted to see my boy and hoped what I had read was true.

Unfortunately, the visit didn't materialize. Judge Cardenas wouldn't let me go. Mr. Ortiz told me they thought I would break down or have a heart attack if I saw David. Judge Cardenas did sign an order giving my son the $13,000 — all the money I had left — and I signed a document to that effect.

Early one morning another article was placed under my door about a visit to my son from Reggie Jackson, the baseball star. Later in the article, however, I discovered some discouraging news: David's kidneys had shut down and he was being assisted by a machine. I showed the article to one of the officers, who allowed me to call the UCI Medical Center. I got one of the nurses, and she said kidney problems were normal in cases like David's and he would probably improve. Suddenly, she asked me why Marie was such a bitch (her words). She told me point blank that she thought Marie had much to do with this tragedy and that her personality showed it. I started to cry, and she reassured me, "Take it easy, Mr. Rothenberg. Your son's going to make it. I know what you must be going through." She promised to let the Orange County Jail know if any important changes in David's condition occurred.

The officer took me into another room and told me that most of the people who worked at the jail didn't think I really wanted to hurt my son, only Marie. I broke down again. He said that he and many others felt that Marie was using the tragedy and looking for media coverage. I told the officer that Marie and John were good people. I didn't want to say anything that might hurt David's recovery or bring out the true facts. He thought I was doing the right thing.

Chris Dee brought me an article saying that my son didn't want to see me anymore. I broke down, and they had to carry me back to my cell. Later Chris asked me for a statement. I said simply, "I love my son." Not long after, Joyce Chapman learned that David had never said such a thing, that it had all been staged by Marie's spokesperson.

I kept to myself in my cell and started to pray for my son. To whom was I praying? I didn't know, but I hoped God would hear me and save my boy.

A lot of mail came in, sometimes in boxes, hundreds and thousands of letters mostly asking me "why?" Everyone wanted to hear my side of the story. I received only four bad letters in all, and those who wrote — over 30,000 — were concerned with the entire situation.

On April 22, 1983, Joyce visited me. During the time I had known her, we had discussed God and Jesus, and Joyce wanted to know if I accepted Jesus. I answered that I was a private individual but had a lot of faith in God. I didn't like it to be in the open because I had nothing to prove to the world. She always talked about Jesus, and I could see the peace in her life.

Joyce gave me some words to repeat to her, and I accepted Jesus. I felt really good about this, but my son was on my mind, and I had to deal with the reality of the situation here on earth. I had committed a terrible act, and although God forgives even the unforgivable, I was shaken by my son's plight and knew it would take time for me to grow in the Lord.

Joyce and her family came to see me often. Her husband, Phil, was such a nice man and a good father, too. I could see in his eyes how much he loved Joyce. Since Phil was working to provide for his family, Joyce came for all of them in spirit.

V

Once again I was having problems with my attorney, Mr. Ortiz. Though I wanted no trial, he set a trial date for September 26, 1983. I called his supervisor and advised him that if Mr. Ortiz didn't take me back to court and let me plead guilty, I would fire him. Within 30 minutes, Mr. Ortiz came to see me. Boy, was he shaken up. I told him I was tired of this circus and wanted to read a statement to the judge, then plead guilty.

In the meantime, Joyce and Phil sent me an attorney, Dan Ellsworth. Dan was a Christian who came to me as a friend. He thought I was doing the right thing by not letting out the real truth, swallowing it, and pleading guilty. He also helped me with the statement I was going to make to Judge James Franks.

I talked to Dan about Mr. Ortiz and how I fought so hard for him just to spend time with me and talk with me. Dan met with Mr. Ortiz and said that he was an excellent attorney — legally — but he thought he was a publicity seeker. Mr. Ortiz told Dan that mine was the best case he ever had with the media and he didn't want to lose this opportunity to get my name known — and his. I asked Dan if he could represent me, but Dan said that the judge probably wouldn't allow it at this point. I wanted Dan to speak for me at my sentencing to explain to the judge feelings that I was not able to convey.

Fortunately, Dan came almost every night, many times with his family, and talked with me about God, my son, you name it. Dan was in so many respects a lifesaver, like the Chapmans. Just being there was so important to me.

On June 7, 1983, David was moved to the Burn Unit of the Shriner's Hospital in Boston to continue his treatment. I was very lonely without him. I still wanted to see my son, or recent pictures of him.

On June 16, 1983, I received a letter from Bishop Duffy, just back from Rome, having spent 15 minutes with Pope John Paul II. He told me that the Holy Father had sent his blessing to me, through him, and was praying for me and my son.

On June 18, 1983, David's birthday, I saw the Orange County Register with headlines that read: "Burned boy receives letter from Reagan; father hears of indirect papal blessing." I was surprised and wondered how they found out about the Pope's blessing. All this publicity made me very nervous. I never knew it would go this far.

Dan, Joyce, Phil, and all of their children came to see me in the evenings after work to lift me up. Because Dan was an attorney, he was the only one allowed to see me at any hour. The others would see me pass and wave to me, then wait for hours as Dan and I talked about tragedy, God, the devil, and many other things. Dan often came at times I didn't expect. He was such a good man and very concerned about me. He gave me excellent advice, both legally and morally, but in the end I made the decisions.

Joyce came every day to spend a half-hour with me, talking about God. She was a rare individual indeed. Dan's wife, Louise, and his daughter Cathy came often, sometimes when I was really down in the dumps. (His daughter Nancy was in college and had little chance to visit.) Once Cathy and I had a two-hour visit, and we cried a lot. It was rare for me to open up to someone like that. If I had a sister, I would want her to be just like Cathy — a lovely, decent lady.

The Buena Park police had taken all the pictures of my son that I had left at the YMCA in San Francisco, and I wanted them back. Dan asked Sergeant Hafdahl for them, but Sergeant Hafdahl had already given them to Marie. Dan was mad as hell. He wanted to sue the Buena Park Police Department, the City of Buena Park, and

Sergeant Hafdahl for punitive damages. He also wanted to bring criminal charges against Sergeant Hafdahl and Marie — Marie for accepting stolen property. I asked Dan to hold off, hoping Marie would return the pictures to me someday. But she never did.

Just before my court date, the Chapmans and the Ellsworths visited me. We prayed together, and all of them agreed that I was doing the right thing. During all the court proceedings, the officers treated me like a human being and also said they thought I was doing the right thing.

VI

On June 24, 1983, I entered Judge Franks' courtroom with my statement in my hand, ready to talk to the judge ... and my son. The only people who knew what I was going to say were Dan Ellsworth and Mr. Ortiz, who would receive a copy of my statement only after I read it. Both he and the district attorney were making a mockery out of the entire tragedy.

I told the judge that so much had been left out of the newspapers, but it would have been dishonest for me to plead not guilty since I did a very bad thing. I said that when I tried to take my son's life and mine, it was just unexplainable. I decided not to disclose to the judge (or my son) the real truth — for my son's emotional well-being. So many things I said that day made me cry. Although the newspapers did not report it, I told the judge, without mentioning their names, how Marie and John had condemned me and verbally abused me for years.

I ended by talking to my son, and only Dan knew I was going to do this. I asked my son's forgiveness and prayed through the grace of the Almighty that he would someday understand. I told David I was wrong to do what I did. Talking to my son in the courtroom made me break down again, and for the first time, Mr. Ortiz showed some compassion and put his arm around me.

The judge ordered the district attorney to say some words to me in the plea-bargaining process. I answered yes to his questions so my guilty plea would be legal and entered on the record. The judge set sentencing for July 29, 1983.

Dan and Joyce both visited me that day. Joyce told me that my son had almost died during a medical procedure in Boston, but was revived. Dan called Boston for me and brought the good news that David was out of danger. Dan said prayers with me and kept me in line. Without his help and concern (and that of the others), I would never have made it.

Bishop Duffy's letters came in regularly, and he, too, lifted my spirits. Dan, Joyce, and Phil all received letters from him, expressing his love for them for caring for me in this time of need.

God, how I prayed for my son and even for Marie, the mother of our child. How I felt her pain seeing our son in his condition. One day I wanted to write to my boy, so I sat down on my bed and wrote him a poem from my heart:

A World Without Tears

Son, I think of a world, a world without tears,
Where we all can live for endless years,
With never a grief, an ache, or a pain,
Nor any hard work exerted in vain.

I think of a world where we can plant a vine,
And sit in its shade and say, "This is mine."
We can live in a house our own hands have made,
And nothing shall molest or make us afraid.

I think of a world without bloodshed or strife
Where no one will dare take another's life,
Where we can unite in lasting peace,
And malice and hatred will forevermore cease.

I think of the earth as a global paradise,
Where mountains and deserts will dazzle your eyes,
With beautiful flowers, shrubbery and trees,
And playful butterflies, songbirds and bees.

I think just as sure as God's word is the truth,
We shall return to the days of our youth,
Our flesh shall become as the flesh of a child,
And the words that we speak will be cheerful and mild.

I think of a world where the lame will leap,
From crag to crag, like a deer or a sheep,
Where none will be maimed, deaf or blind,
And the dumb will sing and speak forth his mind.

I think of a world where each man is a brother,
Not esteeming ourselves above any other,
Where mankind can be friend-to-friend,
In a world without tears that will never end!

A world without tears has always been my dream.
Son, I love you!

Dad

During the five weeks I waited to be sentenced, I received lots of mail. Senator Henry "Scoop" Jackson wrote that he thought I had done the proper thing not to cause my son any more trauma and pain and applauded me for not exposing the events that may have caused the tragedy. He closed by saying, "Do not give up hope, Mr. Rothenberg. One day you will see that your boy will come to you."

Jessica Savitch, a network journalist, wrote of her deep concern that my son was being exploited by my wife and of her respect for my silence. She also told me that her prayers were with me and never to give up hope. Nancy Reagan wrote me a very short letter from the White House: "My thoughts, warm wishes, and friendship are with you, Mr. Rothenberg."

His Holiness Pope John Paul II sent me many letters expressing his prayers for David and me. He told me to remember that God is always with us. Bishop Duffy wrote to the Holy Father, expressing his personal grief over my son's tragedy. He blessed my son and held him in his arms for a few minutes. I could see the pain and hurt Bishop Duffy was going through for David, Marie, and me.

Billy Graham expressed his love and prayers for David and me, hoping one day we will reunite.

Marie's sister wrote and asked me "why?" If she had only known I had problems with Marie and her boyfriend, she said she would have helped me. She thought Marie had caused me to snap. She wanted to be my friend and asked that I write back, but I decided not to. Her letter was dated the day before David appeared on Good Morning, America, and I was not sure if I should continue the correspondence.

Dr. Robert Schuller at the Crystal Cathedral also had Marie and our son on his Sunday television ministry. I cried when I saw Marie and David and thought Dr. Schuller handled the situation decently and sensitively.

Phil Donahue interviewed my wife and son during a program on disfigured persons, and Marie used our son's condition to make some harsh statements about me. I wrote to Phil Donahue, expressing how sad I was to hear that David did not want to see me anymore. Several months later the format of another Donahue show allowed the audience to comment on previous shows. One irate woman lashed out at Marie for allowing my son to be exploited. I received thousands of letters saying that Marie was capitalizing on David's trauma and pain to sell her book. They all wanted to hear my side of the story.

I never forgot the mother of "our son," and I knew nothing would be gained by bringing out the true events. I would never justify that day or the act itself. The act is unforgivable to Marie, and surely to me. Only God can forgive sinners. People can, too, but it seems on most occasions they do not.

I remember once reading an article on how to overcome life's hurts. It said that when you forgive someone for hurting you, you perform spritual surgery inside your soul. And when we heal our memories, we are not playing games or making believe — we come together as family, as one. For me, Jesus (and praying to him) has kept me strong during these times. Praying, especially saying the Lord's Prayer, has given me strength.

A member of Billy Graham's staff wrote to me, and his letter brought me closer to God. A radio minister in Colorado, wrote me about Jesus and suggested that I open my arms to him. Bishop Duffy told me to jump into the arms of Jesus, to know that God forgives all sinners, regardless of their crimes, and to remember that I would be on my way to a better world when I die. He also told me to forgive myself and not to let this tragedy get me down.

A few days before sentencing, Dan spent some time with me to help me put together a final statement. Mr. Ortiz even approved of what I wanted to say. He had me read copies of letters to the judge from the district attorney, Sergeant Hafdahl, and Marie. I told Mr. Ortiz that I felt Mr. Avdeef was going to make a circus out of the sentencing. Then I learned that Marie and John were going to speak at the sentencing. I was shocked that Marie would leave David in Boston. Here I was being used.

I saw Dan just before I went to court on July 29, 1983. I was so glad to see him and grateful that he had lifted me up all these weeks. He told me that the Chapman family would be there and that many other families were very sympathetic.

VII

An officer brought me to the entrance of the courtroom. Mr. Ortiz was to have given me support by walking in with me, but the officer told me he was only interested in all the press. I walked into the full courtroom without him. I had to step over a reporter lying on the floor with a microphone near my seat, and the cameras started to flash in my face. My attorney was just sitting at the table and didn't say anything to me.

The judge asked for Mr. Avdeef's statement, and he put on a show. He thought he was in Hollywood, throwing my son's burn photos on the table in front of Mr. Ortiz and telling the judge his thoughts about what I had done. Mr. Avdeef was shouting at the top of his lungs and making a sideshow out of this tragedy. He and Mr. Ortiz were only concerned about themselves, not my boy.

Mr. Avdeef told the judge that Marie wanted to make a statement before I was sentenced. I was very nervous now and, looking around, saw Marie and John coming to the podium together. I was completely surprised to see John there with her. I noticed them looking at each other with a feeling of relief, as if they finally had their wish of getting me out of the way.

Marie told Judge Franks about our son and his condition. She was looking straight at me, and I saw in her face how content she was that I would be going to prison and finally out of her hair. John held on to Marie's arm, but he never raised his head.

Then the judge allowed me to make a statement. I simply told Marie and John that I forgave them both and asked them to take care of my son.

The statement "I forgive you both" was not to justify my act. I could never justify that day. But only Marie knows why I said this. Marie knows of the 11 taped conversations I have and the attorneys' letters to her, and mine to them, on the custody dispute she claimed never existed. Only Marie knows ...

The judge sentenced me to 13 years at a California correctional facility. He had no alternative to this sentence, and I believe I should have received more, much more — forever.

I was escorted back to the jail, and Dan came immediately to see me. I was crying a lot, not because of the sentence but because I never knew Marie and John would put on a stage presentation in court. It wasn't necessary. I was not angry with them, but rather concerned if John would stay by Marie's side.

(Five months later John left Marie. They had been engaged many times on and off, and I remember a time when John asked me why she was such a difficult person. In my eyes, Marie was a good person and an excellent mother, but she was always condemning and critical of others. I had a serious problem of my own: I always walked away from her mouth, never retaliated verbally, and tried to work it out. Once Marie suggested that we go to a therapist together, but I refused because of my responsibilities to Marie and our son — I was the one flipping the bills. Marie and I are not perfect. We both had had our problems. To her, I'm worse because I committed a terrible act against our son. I don't blame her, I really don't.)

Joyce, Phil, and their two boys came to see me the next day. We all cried together, and I could see the hurt in their faces. The half-hour visits were so short and over before we knew it. Dan came again that same evening, and to my surprise, both the Chapman and the Ellsworth families were there, waving to me. The officers called it the "Rothenberg Fan Club." Dan and I had a long talk. I was scared, not about going to prison but about not ever seeing my son again. Dan told me, like so many others, not to give up, that one day David would want to see me.

On August 2, 1983, I was moved to Chino Prison where inmates are housed for classification evaluation. Dan visited me often to be sure the authorities were not bothering me. He kept me alive in so many ways with his constant encouragements. I told Dan the staff was okay; it was the inmates who were the problem. They talked about other inmates' crimes just to get away from their own problems and harrassed anyone whose case had received publicity.

Joyce came to see me every week. I have never met a mother who was as strong as Joyce. This woman just remained by my side.

She was the key to my holding on all these months. She lifted me up, talked about God, and wrote to me daily; and she and her family continue to write and visit me to this day.

I asked Dan for recent pictures of my son. I couldn't get over this tragedy and needed to come to grips with his present condition. He finally brought three photos, and I was devastated when I saw them. I broke down and cried, and Dan held me and talked with me for a long time.

I wanted to be alone, and it was a bad night for me. I couldn't get over my son's condition. I had never seen his burns and never knew it was that bad. God, I did a very bad thing! I never imagined it would be like this. I didn't even know what third degree burns were like. No one told me.

On September 29, 1983, I was transported by bus to Soledad Prison where I was housed in a protected unit with inmates who were in for various types of crimes. At first I thought I would have difficulties with them (and I did at first with a few), but most realized it would serve no purpose to bother me. I got to know many of the inmates. On the whole, they were manipulators and informers. In my experience, many inmates would sell out their own families to gain release; they would certainly inform on another inmates to shorten their sentences. Every inmate I ever met claimed he was innocent. They manipulate their attorneys and their families, get drugs into the prison, commit homosexual activities on the tier, and make wine. Many inmates use the church by attending services and trying to get a good report from the minister, just to manipulate the system. So few inmates let their time serve them, using it for good and not for evil.

At Soledad, many of the correctional officers, staff, and ministers have uplifted me during my personal fight within myself. Natalie Carpenter, a prison administrator, has been a real buddy by just stopping by and asking how I'm doing. A bishop from Monterey County has written and befriended me during my incarceration and has lifted my spirits in prayer. Ministers of various faiths have visited me and supported me emotionally when my hopes seemed to wane. Anthony Sardo, a businessman, and Father John, a Roman Catholic priest, have both helped me.

All know how private I am about my faith—I have always been quiet and shy—but I know my faith is strong and growing. I've never used faith in God to get away from what I am going through with my son's plight, but I have come closer to God. I know I have jumped into Jesus' arms, and this is the most important aspect now. I have asked God to forgive me, and I know that God has forgiven me for all the sins in my life. I can feel it. Praying gives me much peace and strength when I have conversations with God.

Now I wonder about something else — my son and his forgiveness. I love my son. He was all that I struggled for in life. I think about him then and now, and it deeply hurts. But he's still my son, and I love him.

I don't know if I'll ever see David again, but I won't give up. I know it is totally up to him if we reunite. I will spend the rest of my life working and saving for David, and my only prayer is before I pass on into another life — heaven, I hope — I will see my son again. Without him, my life, my heart, and my arms will be empty and lonely. I have asked God to enable us to see each other again, maybe even with his mother, Marie. Although I know this is almost impossible now, with God anything is possible.

A true love that heals will never lose its power, and as a Christian, I know we can reunite through forgiveness and understand we all are human beings under God. I know I have been a terrible sinner, and although I have given myself to Jesus freely, I must also accept and realize where my feet take hold — on this earth — until God takes me. I pray that David and I will reunite again, with love and forgiveness.

I love you, Son! ■

Analysis III
Jack Wilson

In Charles' account of his crime, he gives no indication of any thoughts about God or judgment, and indeed in an interview he denied having such thoughts. Again his unmet needs to belong and to sense esteem emerge. After he found out that David was in the UCI Medical Center Burn Unit, the only words in his writings that suggest any moral sense are, *"I knew I had done a very bad thing. I took my anger out on my son, an anger I never knew before, an anger I never thought would come to this. I knew David might die. I was scared and didn't know what to do or whom to turn to."* Not only do his remarks suggest a shallow conscience, but they also indicate that his concern was more with himself than his son.

After flying to San Francisco and checking into the YMCA under the alias of "David Love," he walked for hours, brooding that he only wanted to shut Marie's mouth. The next day he anonymously sent a telegram to Marie because, he says, *"I didn't want David to be alone!"* He punctuates with the exclamation point as if to indicate his deep concern for his son. And his concern was no doubt as deep as it could be for one who, as a child, had never connected at a deep level with a parent figure.

During the week after the burning, he continued to lie about his identity and to run from the authorities. While on the run, he called Bishop Duffy. Charles' stated reason was that he was lonely, scared, and very confused, and he just wanted to hear Duffy's voice. This behavior fits the pattern that recurs in Charles' life: he turned to religion to meet certain inner needs.

In describing his arrest, Charles maintains his established concept about himself that he is, at the core, a nice person and concerned about others. He is quick to point out that the arresting officers did not harm him and even showed him sympathy. He reports the remark of one officer who said, "You should have done this to your wife. ...I don't think you meant to hurt your son." He portrays his concern for Marie and David by his telling Sergeant Hafdahl about $13,000 in his drawer at the YMCA that he wanted to be given to *"my son and Marie."* This preoccupation with money in a drawer at a time when his son was fighting for his life seems inane. But Charles did not have much of a moral frame of reference.

Charles was introduced to fundamentalist evangelical Christianity by Joyce Chapman who visited him in prison. He remembers thinking that he hoped *"...she wouldn't shove God into my face, like some already had done since this tragedy."* This statement is striking and may be a manifestation of arrogance. He distanced himself from his own horrid crime by calling it *"this tragedy,"* and asserted his own right to privacy. But he responded to her apparent compassion for him as a person. He tells of a sense of spiritual lostness, saying that he was praying for David, but that he didn't know to whom he was praying and that he only hoped God would hear and save David.

Through Joyce, Charles *"accepted Jesus."* He reports it as Joyce's giving him *"some words to repeat to her,"* an action that fits the pattern of evangelism followed by many evangelical Christians who give some instruction about the gospel and encourage a person to receive Christ by repeating a prayer. The purpose is to cause people to understand that they need to exercise personal, conscious faith in Jesus Christ, his atoning sacrifice, and his resurrection. When rightly understood, this means that the person has experienced a kind of spiritual resurrection. Confident that sins have been forgiven by God on the basis of the atonement of Christ, confident that God's love has been received, confident that death really is an entrance into glory, one is able to move forward within an entirely different spiritual frame of reference.

Charles admits that he felt *"really good about this,"* but that his son was on his mind and he *"...knew it would take time ... to grow in the Lord."* If uncoached, this remark is indicative of one who has connected with a notion of spiritual growth presented in the New Testament: "Like newborn babies, crave pure spiritual milk, so that by it you may grow up in your salvation, now that you have tasted that the Lord is good."[5] Charles calls his act of burning David *"terrible,"* and indicates an awareness of God's forgiveness, but he does not give clear evidence of associating his own crime with the cross of Jesus Christ. From my perspective as a gospel minister, I believe that the only way Charles can truly accept the fact of his terrible crime, without continuing in a state of constant drowning anguish, is to comprehend that his crime was indeed judged and paid for on the cross.

The involvement of fundamentalist evangelical Christians continued. Charles depended on these relationships, especially his relationship with the attorney, Dan Ellsworth. Charles writes that Dan approved of his decision to hide the *"real truth,"* but Charles may simply have used this self-perceived restraint in not telling his side of the story about his disputes with Marie over visitation rights as a means to boost his own esteem.

Charles writes freely of the support and prayers of Bishop Duffy and many others who contacted him during his incarceration. His recounting of the support of those from fundamentalist or evangelical Christian traditions does not seem to be very different in

---

[5] I Peter 2.2, 3.

character from his reports of assistance offered to him by those from the Episcopal and Roman Catholic traditions. Charles may simply have been responding to those who reached out to him, but this experience echoes the uncritical vacillation of his earlier life. His spiritual experience with Joyce does not seem to have prejudiced him against Roman Catholicism, a prejudice not uncommon among those who turn to a more fundamentalist form of Christianity. This again may be indicative of a lack of cognitive theological development.

Charles writes about his crime from a spiritual context, claiming that he can never justify his act, that it is unforgivable on a human level, that only God can forgive. Yet he fails to associate his crime or God's forgiveness with Christ's death on the cross. Charles knows he has done something wrong, but he does not seem to have the sense of justice within himself to comprehend the moral depth of his crime. He reports receiving spiritual strength from prayer, but his progression beyond the superficial piety of his early years seems limited. He claims that he has never used his faith in God to escape the earthly consequences of his act towards David, but he has asked God to forgive him and knows that God has. As Charles concludes his written story, he appears to believe that he will go to heaven when he dies. Yet his understanding of the gospel seems shallow. None of his assertions about God's forgiveness seem to connect with the notion of Christ's sacrifice for sin, a basic doctrine in the Christian gospel. He does not appear to have a strong distaste for sins for which Christ died. He is very upset by the suffering he has caused his son, and that seems to be the extent of it.

When I interviewed Charles, I questioned him about his understanding of the cross. I found no real insights into sin and guilt. He made the kind of remarks one would expect from a kid in Sunday School. Even after carefully reviewing the teaching of II Corinthians 5:21, which describes the transfer of human guilt to Christ and the merits of Christ's goodness to human beings, opening the way for a right relationship with God, I did not feel that he had actually seized on its significance. He told me he understood that he had been "*vindicated by Jesus,*" but I was not convinced that he was really impressed with this concept. This apparent shallowness would not be unexpected in one whose conscience was developed insufficiently in childhood. Charles' view of God consists primarily of metaphors denoting one who helps people in trouble. The cross of Christ does not appear to be central to his personal theology.

Charles presents himself as having been "*born again*" through the ministry of Joyce Chapman, yet he told me that he credits Bishop Duffy for his spiritual growth. Most Christians within a fundamental evangelical tradition would find this statement an anomaly, since those responsible for spiritual growth also usually lead a person to a saving knowledge of Jesus Christ.

It is common for people to think that convicts "use" religion as a means for lessening their sentences or as a means for gaining self-esteem. Charles himself is wary of using religion to win the sympathy of others. He told me that he doesn't talk openly a great deal about his relationship with God, in part out of fear that others may think he is insincere, even though he usually puts his best foot forward with people, presenting himself as he believes others want him to be. I found it intriguing that his discussions with me about matters of Christianity were rather void of biblical or theological reference.

Charles told me that he reads the Bible for 14 to 16 hours every day, that he was starting his fourth time of reading through it. When I asked him for his favorite biblical passage, he indicated Psalm 23, a passage filled with pastoral images and notions of care and help, with no reference to guilt and forgiveness. This choice is one more sign that he has not learned to think through his crime from the perspective of the cross.

At the conclusion of my discussions with Charles, I asked him this question: "When you're judged, and you stand before God and God says, 'Why should I let you into heaven?' what will you say?" Charles answered, *"At this particular stage, I'd say I've changed. I try to follow the commandments. I've sinned. I've become a better person. I'm not sure how I would totally respond to that."*

I further asked him about how the cross factored in. He responded, *"Well, Jesus died so that we may live. I tell you that I have read about a lot of people. But the story of Jesus ... his whole 33 years, he's probably the greatest man that ever lived. And he's been condemned too. They have what they call anti-christs. I think it's terrible. I hope that when I die I will be taken into heaven. I hope that all my sins can be forgiven, but it's up to me now ... the change that's come about me over the last six years...."*

I tried to press him with the gospel teaching that the basis on which a person is made acceptable before God is not in one's own righteousness, but rather on the basis of the righteousness that's given as a gift. He claimed to understand and added, *"...but we have to take that gift and use it properly.... I am fortunate that I am not a revengeful person, especially to those that dislike me. I don't hate people who have done anything to me. My life, when I get out, I hope to walk in Jesus' path. I just don't know where it's going to lead me. I'd like to do a lot of good for other people. I don't know what. I just ... am scared, I don't know where my life will be."*

Charles' comments do not lead me to believe that he has a solid grasp on the grace of God offered to all through Christ. Forgiveness on the day of judgment is not contingent upon one's own merits, but upon the merits freely offered to all by Jesus Christ. If Charles can grasp this concept and understand that he is made acceptable to God in Christ, he will be able to accept himself, and even know how better to live with the memory of his crime. He will understand that the ultimate blame for his crime has been transferred to Christ. This understanding will probably heighten, rather than diminish the wrongness of his crime in his mind. But even though there are earthly consequences to his actions, he will have the theology to help him handle the guilt feelings with which he will continue to struggle.

Charles' religious experience shows several things to the church. First, it demonstrates the importance of the church's outreach to those in need. Charles was helped many times through his life by the church and religious persons, all to their credit. His experience also shows that the church's outreach must include positive teaching about handling the pressures of life, including the message of morality. Society gives mixed moral messages. A baseball player may be suspended for a month for using drugs and suspended for life for betting. I believe that the church cannot simply "reach out" with a meal to those who are hungry. It must teach about right and wrong. About responsible living. About responsible parenting.

If Charles heard such messages from the church and religious persons through his life, they made little, if any, impression. When life's pressures became too great, he was able to commit a horrendous crime and hurt his own child, giving no thought to the moral wrongness of it. Charles' religious experience caused him intuitively to reach out to the church when he felt alone, but nothing caused him to reach out for help with his family problems. Counseling services certainly are available through many religious organizations, but Charles just didn't think that way.

I don't know if his understanding has yet gone beyond simply feeling terrible for what he did because of the pain it caused another human being. It may have. And it certainly must if he is going to grow in his Christian faith and adjust to life in a society that will always have the reflex to reject him, if it finds out about him. I don't know if he is fully aware of his lack of wisdom for life, beyond just knowing he needs assistance in finding a job and a place to live. He needs to learn that wisdom for handling life can be accessed through many local churches, religious organizations, and literature.

If Charles has truly had the kind of conversion experience that is talked about in the Christian gospel, his life will be much different when he is released from prison. I doubt that he will ever hurt anyone again. I believe his crime itself - the memory of it and the pain it has caused - will itself keep him from ever hurting anyone. But remember that Charles was a thief. And Charles would go to almost any length to satisfy his needs for self-esteem and to belong. If he is truly converted, he will have grounds for self-respect that earthly circumstances cannot take away: he has become one with Jesus Christ. "Therefore, if anyone is in Christ, he is a new creation; the old has gone, the new has come! All this is from God.... God made him who had no sin to be sin for us, so that in him we might become the rightousness of God."[6] ■

---

[6] II Corinthians 5:17, 18a, 21.

Andrew Savicky: Child Abuse Formula

All human beings are complex mixtures of needs and strengths and weaknesses that, when in balance, allow them to function "normally," at least according to society's definition. It is only when the needs tilt out of balance with the resources to meet them that trouble, such as the impulse or decision to abuse a child, occurs.

Charles Rothenberg provides valuable information on the makeup of an individual who could commit a brutal act of child abuse. In this case Charles himself is a willing participant in sharing information about his background and allowing insights into his personality profile. By studying Charles' story, we can develop, refine, and illustrate a formula for child abuse that can be used to analyze particular parental characteristics and behavior to prevent what then becomes predictable child abuse.

$$\text{The formula:} \quad \frac{(D + P - T + V) \times C}{S + Cn} = A$$

D = Personality disorder
P = Passive dependent needs
T = Treatment
V = Trusting victim
C = Circumstances and timing
S = Spiritual resources
Cn = Conscience
A = Child abuse

In other words: when an explosive combination of a person with untreated personality disorders and passive dependent needs in close proximity to a trusting victim is multiplied by just the right circumstances and timing, abuse will probably occur, unless these factors are mitigated by the person's spiritual resources and conscience. Changing any of the elements of this equation, of course, changes the outcome; but recognizing what lies behind abusive behavior is the first step in preventing it. Charles Rothenberg's story aids our understanding.

Personality disorder: Evidence indicates that Charles suffered primarily from a masochistic personality disorder. He tended to

119

remain in relationships in which others exploited him, abused him, or took advantage of him, even when he had opportunities to alter the situation or terminate the relationship. He often felt the need to sacrifice his own interests for those of others. Although he knew the consequences of his criminal acts, he nonetheless stole in order to help others. But when others tried to help him, he usually chose not to be a burden to them or to be obligated to them. He seemed unable to say no.

Although Charles did not complain directly of feeling unappreciated, testing and interviewing reveal that he indeed thought he was very much unappreciated. Whenever positive feedback was offered to Charles, he responded by feeling undeserving or worrying about his inability to measure up to the new responsibilities of success, and thus he could not accept it. This behavior may be traced to his childhood feelings of inadequacy.

Charles was often preoccupied by the worst aspects of the past and the present and pessimistic about the future. He felt *"something inside"* that told him things would go wrong. The ultimate sabotage of his own intended goals came with his abuse of David. His goal was to have a positive relationship with the one person who trusted him and held him up as a hero, but Charles made David his worst enemy.

Antisocial individuals often behave outside of society's accepted norms, mores, and laws, and Charles also exhibited this personality profile. He was dishonest many times throughout his life. For example, he probably fabricated aspects of his own story; he had an inconsistent work history; he repeatedly performed antisocial acts that led to his arrest; and ultimately he committed his crime against David. He usually justified his antisocial behavior with a goal or a purpose: he stole because someone else needed help.

In addition, Charles was dependent, preferring to have others make most or all of his major life decisions. He remained in relationships with people who mistreated him and agreed with people even when he believed they were wrong simply to avoid disturbing the relationship for fear of being alone. He constantly sought reassurance, approval, and praise, even to the point of criminal behavior to get others to like him.

Passive dependent needs: As a passive dependent individual, Charles placed a great deal of responsibility on others so that they would feel obligated to fulfill his needs. However, since he was unable to express his needs, he indirectly avoided problems and left many questions unanswered. He simply walked away from problems and did not handle them directly.

Charles was often unassertive in interacting with aggressive people, with only a few exceptions. When he did deal with a problem assertively, such as in his confrontation with John, he was able to reach a somewhat satisfactory conclusion. By dealing passively with Marie, he created a victim in David where none needed to exist. He was dependent upon David to resolve the problem; thus David became part of the problem, when, in fact, he was not the problem at all.

Charles often referred to important people in his life as those who would be responsible for him. They became father figures in place of the father he never had. His feelings were often hurt by criticism or disapproval, and he had very few close friends. David was one person he could count on; however, Charles ended that dependency by making David the victim of his frustration and anger.

Treatment: Whenever a personality disorder and passive dependent needs exist together, treatment is likely to decrease the chances of these two variables causing a problem. Alternatives for treatment include a pharmacological approach, behavioral treatment, directive and nondirective therapies, and family therapy.

Although Charles may not be a completely dependent individual, he was prone to depression and may have benefitted from antidepressants. These medications can also lessen masochistic personality traits. Behavioral treatment could have helped Charles develop the life skills he lacked, such as social skills and assertiveness, and could have taught him how to communicate more effectively and to control anxiety and stress. Had Charles known how to communicate more directly with Marie, he might not have used David as a means of dealing with her. Psychotherapy would have allowed Charles to talk about his life and learn to deal with the problems that burdened him. If Charles had been willing to enter family therapy with Marie, how different his life might have been.

Trusting victim: Most children involved in their parents' struggle for control are unable to understand the conflict and incapable of communicating their concern and fear of losing one or both parents. As the intensity of the dispute gains momentum, the innocent child becomes a possession to be manipulated by each parent. When one of the parents senses failure, the trusting child is at risk of being used as a tool to strike back. In this case, David was the trusting victim who believed that Charles would do nothing to hurt him. For Charles, David provided the means for dealing with his problem indirectly. The problem was not with David, but David was part of the solution because he was trusting, innocent, and available — like many other victims of child abuse.

Circumstances and timing: Given a person with an untreated personality disorder and passive dependent needs together with an available victim, circumstances such as pressure or stress not only increase but multiply the possibility of child abuse. Charles felt cornered when he learned that Marie intended to terminate his visitation rights with David. In his mind, he had no alternative but to get back at all the people whom he had never confronted or communicated with in a genuine manner. David represented those on whom Charles wanted to take his revenge, a total retaliation for all the people who had affected him adversely. So many difficult factors gathered at once that he had no means to deal with, and all he could do was to lash out.

Spiritual resources: One denominator that can lessen the impact of the explosive possibilities of the numerator of this equation is spiritual resources, which could be any form of religious or spiritual investment but particularly a belief system that enables a person to respond to God. Those who have a strong belief in the existence of God and desire to relate meaningfully with God tend to have a perspective on life that greatly influences their responses to stress or pressure: they have resources on which to draw for strength and support that can mitigate even the worst circumstances. If Charles had been a more spiritually committed person, his spiritual resources could have helped him better to manage the exigencies of his life and would surely have lessened the likelihood of his ever committing such a horrid act.

Conscience: Conscience is that inner sense that evaluates actions based on an internalized code of ethics. Such a code of ethics derives from one's background and arouses feelings about the choices one makes, with strong negative feelings tending to inhibit antisocial action. Charles' conscience was not well developed, and he had a long history of being unable to make appropriate choices. Thus, when faced with what for him was an unbearable situation, unmoderated by any spiritual support, he could not rely on his conscience to alter events. Had the variables of strong spiritual resources and a well-developed conscience been present, Charles would have had significant conscious reason to think before he acted and probably would not have carried out his crime.

Abuse: Child abuse appears in many guises, but most would agree that Charles' act of burning David was one of the cruelest forms of brutality and child abuse that has ever occurred. This formula, though developed from information about an isolated incident, can be an instrument to assess behavior that can lead parents and children down a fearful path.

Most parents have tales to tell of times when they could have crossed the line and harmed a child. If the equation had been weighted with more negative factors, if the circumstances and timing had been just right, the outcome could have been different. Fortunately, most parents are able to recognize the potential danger in a situation and take steps to remedy it. ■

Harry Gaynor: Summary

There is no easy solution to the complex problem of child abuse. Violence inflicted on children, both physically and emotionally, has not received adequate attention or funding. Much talk exists about the problem, but the lack of commitment to remedies by both the public and private sectors results in slow and inconsistent progress. The incidence of reported child abuse is growing dramatically since the public has become more sensitized to this national social problem. According to the U.S. Department of Health and Human Services, cases of child abuse and neglect increased 66 percent from 1980 to 1986.

Dollars alone will not solve our nation's problems involving battered children, but we cannot afford to ignore the cries of hundreds of thousands of these children every year. Politicians and large governmental human service agencies responsible for the safety, health, and welfare of abused and neglected children are spending huge sums annually, attempting to respond to a massive social problem from the top down. These agencies too often have their hands tied by budgetary restraints and are asked to do more with less.

We need new, innovative ideas to improve all child protective service programs. Training in research and forensic methodology in evaluating suspected child abuse is needed to determine if a child has indeed been abused or neglected. Medical schools and the American College of Emergency Physicians can take the lead. Aggressive parenting skills programs for high school and college students are essential, with an emphasis on students residing in densely populated, low-income urban areas where a disproportionate number of burns in children are suspected of being the result of abuse or neglect.

May all who are involved on the cutting edge of child abuse prevention take Charles Rothenberg's challenge to heart. Our children have a right to a safe environment where they can grow and thrive. ∎

Appendix
Andrew Savicky

I   <u>Human Figure Drawings</u>

In the field of psychology, the use of drawings has become an adjunct to aid in accurate diagnoses. Drawing also serves to improve communication and rapport between therapist and patient because of its simple nature. People will draw because it is nonthreatening. For the examiner, drawing is a brief, easy-to-administer exercise. It leads to vast interpretations and can be helpful in counseling or psychotherapy. Drawings become vehicles for expression of fears, needs, and fantasies, or can even form therapeutic goals. They can also be avenues for dealing with frustrations and impulses in the process of developing communication skills that will elevate a person's self-image.

Drawings are reflections of the individual's emotional conflicts and are thus emotional indicators. The therapist can analyze these emotional indictors or signs by the quality of the drawn figure or line quality (e.g., broken, smooth, sketchy), and integration of body parts and their proportions. Some body parts may be expected, such as eyes, nose, feet, and neck, and omissions of these details may be important in the final analysis. Specific features (large or small head, cut-off hands) often point to specific problem areas and serve to indicate a direction for therapy.

Charles' drawings are fairly primitive compared to his ability to articulate, and they demonstrate an unwillingness to share his feelings. He doesn't give much. His simple drawings probably attempt to camouflage feelings of anger, aggression, fear, and helplessness, as well as an inability to ask for help or accept it when offered.

In Charles' drawing of himself (figure 1), the eyes are empty, communicating nothing or perhaps holding in aggressive, angry feelings. The lack of arms may be indicative of guilt over hostility or sexuality. The face itself is happy as if to project that everything is OK, contradicting his feelings.

In the drawing of his family (figure 2), Charles is the largest figure, the most influential, though small in relation to the size of the paper, suggesting insecurity, withdrawal, depression, and feelings of inadequacy. A big figure in relation to the family may suggest poor inner controls and expansiveness, going beyond the scope of responsibility in the family. The drawing of David is identical except for the size and shows David as an extension of himself, a continuation of his masochistic beliefs. The drawing of Marie is different from David and Charles because her eyes have pupils, indicating that one knows where one stands with her.

Drawings of the home tend to reflect interpersonal relationships within the home. Again, Charles' drawing (figure 3) is primitive, offering few details. The house lacks a chimney, which may mean a lack of psychological warmth or conflicts with significant male figures. No sidewalk leads to the door, making the house unapproachable.

Drawings of trees are often associated with one's life role and one's capabilities in obtaining rewards from the environment — a blooming biography. Charles' large tree (figure 4) may illustrate aggressive tendencies, and the exaggerated emphasis on the crown of the tree may indicate inhibited emotional feelings. ■

Figure 1

Figure 2

Figure 3

Figure 4

II   Complete the Sentence Test

Name: Charles David Rothenberg
Sex: Male   Age: 49
Date: 6/17/89   Place: California Correctional Facility

Instructions: Do all the sentences as quickly as you can!

1.   Athletics- *"I like, especially basketball."*
2.   My feelings- *"are sometimes on edge."*
3.   I feel pain- *"deeply when I see others hurt another."*
4.   My brain- *"is always thinking."*
5.   Females- *"see me attractive, yet they don't know me as me."*
6.   It is not possible for me to- *"lose."*
7.   I worry about- *"death and what happens after."*
8.   Mom- *"is a difficult job."*
9.   I am angry- *"most is not having anything to do."*
10.   Guys- *"are young men growing up."*
11.   I feel bad about- *"doing this bad."*
12.   I want to learn- *"more about myself and life."*
13.   I enjoy- *"helping people, especially senior citizens
        and children."*
14.   Going out- *"is fun at times."*
15:     If possible- *"want to see my son and his mother again,
        but it's up to them."*
16.   If only- *"I could start my life again."*
17.   In school- *"I was okay, but not the best of my potential."*
18.   What bothers me- *"more is when I see people hurt others."*
19.   I'm good when- *"I'm not tired."*
20.   I require- *"a family."*
21.   I was glad when- *"I even witnessed seeing my son born."*
22.   In the house- *"I enjoy having a cup of coffee and watching TV."*
23.   Before I sleep- *"I first say my prayers and go to sleep."*
24.   The positive- *"is yet to come."*
25.   Human beings- *"are wonderful when they're kind."*
26.   Inside I am- *"happy at times, sad others."*
27.   In school- *I was a fairly good student."*
28.   As a kid- *"I loved to play basketball."*
29.   Other people- *"seem to be more happier than I."*
30.   Did poorly- *"in my high school grades at Taft."*
31.   Tomorrow- *"looks great!"*
32.   Going out- *"is okay, but I'm very picky."*
33.   I despise- *"nothing."*
34.   My problem is- *"with the room I'm now in, is that it's cold."*
35.   Dad- *"I never met my natural dad."*
36.   My biggest concern is- *"what my life will become."*

130

Analysis of Sentence Completion Test

Another tool for psychologists is a projective technique in which the person completes unfinished sentences. This test is a further development of the word association test in which a person responds to a stimulus word with the first word that comes to mind. The use of incomplete sentences usually elicits significant material because it affords freedom of response and makes it difficult for people to know what constitutes a "good or right" or "bad and wrong" response.

There is no formal scoring system, but the examiner is alert for responses that are unusual, long, overaccurate, tension-producing, intense, and overly-colored. Even erasures or omissions may be significant. What is learned can indicate a direction for therapy.

This test is a chance for Charles to talk about his feelings without an opportunity to hide the feelings and ideals that he doesn't otherwise communicate. Some of his answers reveal contradictions between what he thinks and what he does; they point to his problem of behaving not because of what he is thinking but because of other circumstances. *"What bothers me more is when I see people hurt others"* and *"I feel pain deeply when I see others hurt another"* are examples.

Charles' need for people to be dependent on him is evident in his statement *"I enjoy helping people, especially senior citizens and children."* Charles doesn't like stressful situations, and these two nonthreatening segments of the population are the least likely to confront him or make him uncomfortable.

"My brain is always thinking" expresses Charles' mistrustful approach to others in his tendency to try to determine what others are thinking or doing at the expense of spontaneity. He doesn't want to reveal himself because his thoughts and feelings may not be acceptable, a defense mechanism that manifests his passive dependent needs.

Charles seems to be committed to being unhappy. *"Other people seem to be more happier than I"* shows that Charles probably feels that because his past was unhappy, the future will be unhappy, too. His fatalistic approach will all but ensure it.

"My feelings are sometimes on edge" is a statement that makes a good starting point for therapy. Charles sometimes reveals uncontrollable feelings and in therapy could learn to understand his behavior and release tension with insight. ■

Harry Gaynor

Stress and Violence: Violence is not new in our society; however, violence against children under emotionally stressful circumstances can be identified with a measure of predictability. Fortunately, most parents are able to exhibit restraint, to walk away when they are angry, to stop short of striking their children, thus sparing a child from becoming an innocent target for violence. Only through education and awareness of the "red flags" signaling imminent abuse will the senseless violence inflicted upon children be resolved or significantly reduced.

The following lists represent circumstances in which a child may be at risk of physical or emotional insults. Any one or combination of these can be enough, when triggered, to push a parent to the edge.

I Parental Factors in Child Abuse

A variety of factors contribute to parental stress levels, and abusive parents hold many traits in common.

The parent may be:
young
emotionally immature
unable to cope with stress
depressed
unable to view the chid as an individual with rights
unaware of the child's needs
lacking in knowledge and experience
overwhelmed by feelings of worthlessness, fear, and anger
abused as a child
perfectionistic
a substance abuser
unemployed
poor
lacking family support
socially isolated
separated/divorced
caring for elderly, dependent relative(s)

mother:
inadequate
unable to mother the child
father:
aggressive
jealous of the child due to loss of the wife's attention.

Other factors that can also influence the parent may include having:
had an uncaring mother
a poor self-concept
low self-esteem
unrealistic expectations of the child
history of domestic violence
inadequate housing
reduced income
several children
recently moved or planning to move
physical/mental illness
recent death in the family.

II   Risk Factors in Abused Children

Children at high risk of abuse may share some of the following characteristics:

unwanted
premature
low birth weight
failure to thrive
disappointing to the parent (e.g., sex, birth defects, appearance)
in need of special care due to ill health
difficult to nurture
mentally/physically handicapped
hyperactive
a difficult child
a twin
undergoing dramatic developmental changes
(e.g., adolescence)

Call for Help

If you can identify with any of the "red flags" listed or if you are concerned that someone you know may be at risk of harming a child, call the toll-free number below most appropriate to your need.

Childhelp USA - 1-800-4-A-CHILD

Provides professional counseling and crisis intervention services on a 24-hour daily basis. Will, if necessary, advise on legal issues and referrals to child protective agencies.

Parents Anonymous - 1-800-421-0353

Provides 24-hour daily referral service to closest Parents Anonymous group in caller's area or to other appropriate source for help.

Write for Help

**National Burn Victim Foundation
308 Main Street
Orange, New Jersey 07050
(201) 731-3112**

If a parent or guardian of a child believes he or she has been falsely accused of abuse by causing a burn injury to a child, or if you know of a case where you believe the abuser has not been charged, you can contact the Foundation's Burned Child Team to determine whether professional intervention is applicable.

Update on Charles Rothenberg

On January 24, 1990 Charles Rothenberg was paroled; he was released from prison under a cloak of security. Few in prison knew of his destination. There was an outcry from the public and the press. Charles was considered to be one of the nation's ten most unwanted persons.

His son, David, held a press conference to tell the public how he felt about his father, whom he refers to as "Charles." "He's a sick man," said David, "I want to know where he is . . . I believe he will try again."

Charles responded in a press notice that he had watched his son on TV and heard his statement. He wanted David to know that he would respect his wishes.

Charles' location has not been disclosed. Rumor had it that he was in Oakland, California. Protests immediately arose from politicians and the public. No one wanted him in their town.

The State of California will spend more than $600,000 in three years on security measures to protect Charles from harm and to assure David and his mother that they are safe. David keeps a loaded BB gun at his bedside to protect him from his father, giving him a sense of security.

Twenty-two parole agents have been assigned to Charles. Two agents at a time are with him around the clock. Charles wears a voice-activated detector by which he is tested hourly; in addition, he wears an electronic bracelet monitoring his whereabouts.

In a telephone call Charles Rothenberg said, "I am still not free; the only difference is I have a larger backyard to wander in." Is this the last we will hear of Charles Rothenberg? We think not.

About the Authors

Harry J. Gaynor founded the National Burn Victim Foundation in 1974. He developed a forensic system in 1975 to determine whether a child's burn injuries are the result of abuse, neglect, or accident; and he has evaluated over 900 cases of suspected child abuse by burning. Qualified as an expert witness in Superior Courts in New Jersey and New York, he is also a consultant and evaluator for state social service and criminal justice agencies.

Jack Wilson has been senior pastor of the Calvary Evangelical Free Church in Essex Fells, New Jersey, since 1982. He holds degrees from Northeastern Bible College (B.R.E.), Biblical Theological Seminary (M.Div.), and Drew University (M.Phil., Ph.D.). For 15 years, a significant part of his ministry has been in pastoral counseling.

Andrew Savicky received his Ph.D. degree from the University of Pennsylvania and also holds degrees from Seton Hall University and Montclair State College. A diplomate of the American Board of Medical Psychotherapists and the American Academy of Pain Management, Dr. Savicky is psychology director and principal clinical psychologist at Southern State Correctional Facility in Delmont, New Jersey.